# Proclamation
# of the Gospel

# Proclamation of the Gospel

## for the Salvation of Humankind

Catherine Gunsalus González

Witherspoon Press
Louisville, Kentucky

© 2003 Witherspoon Press, Presbyterian Church (U.S.A.), Louisville, Kentucky

Quotations from the *Book of Order* and the *Book of Confessions* of the Presbyterian Church (U.S.A.) are used with permission of the Office of the General Assembly of the Presbyterian Church (U.S.A.).

Unless otherwise noted, Scripture quotations are from the New Revised Standard Version of the Bible, copyright © 1989 by the Division of Christian Education of the National Council of the Churches of Christ in the U.S.A. Used by permission.

Witherspoon Press gratefully acknowledges the support of the Offices of the General Assembly and Theology and Worship for the publication of *Proclamation of the Gospel*.

*Book interior and cover design by Jeanne Williams*

First edition

Published by Witherspoon Press
Louisville, Kentucky

Web site address: www.pcusa.org/witherspoon

PRINTED IN THE UNITED STATES OF AMERICA

02 03 04 05 06 07 08 09 10 11—10 9 8 7 6 5 4 3 2 1

Library of Congress
Cataloging in Publication Division
101 Independence Ave., S.E.
Washington, D.C. 20540-4320

**Library of Congress Cataloging-in-Publication Data**

González, Catherine Gunsalus.
   Proclamation of the Gospel for the salvation of humankind / Catherine
G. González.—1st ed.
      p. cm.
Includes bibliographical references.
   ISBN 1-57153-043-6
   1. Evangelistic work—Presbyterian Church (U.S.A.). 2. Presbyterian
Church (U.S.A.) Great ends of the church. I. Title.
BX8969.5.G66 2003
266'.5137—dc21                                    2003010667

# Contents

# Foreword

I grew up in a large Presbyterian church in Memphis, Tennessee. It was clearly our congregation's assumption that if you built a large Presbyterian church, they would come. No more. It was our assumption that as a church with a passion for mission, living in a church society, we had to be concerned mainly about our missionaries overseas. The mission frontier was in Africa, Asia, and Latin America. No more. Now the mission frontier is at the doorsteps of our church. It was assumed that most Presbyterian churches were middle-sized, middle-class, Euro-American institutions. No more.

The world and the society in which we live are much different from the world and the society in which I grew up. Today, we are a church seeking to do mission within a secular culture with no shared religious beliefs or values and in which there soon will be no dominant racial ethnic group. And an increasing number of us in the Presbyterian Church do not have Presbyterian roots or background.

Yet, as Presbyterians, we have the gift of a common faith—expressed in our Confessions—and the gift of a common mission—expressed primarily in the first four chapters of our Form of Government. These four chapters set forth our whole life as a church with Jesus Christ as the living head of the church. They give the church what I call its mission statement in the Great Ends of the Church. It is to the first Great End of the Church—"the proclamation of the gospel for the salvation of humankind"—that my friend and colleague Catherine González directs our attention in this book in a timely and articulate way.

Dr. González draws upon her expertise in church history to provide the solid grounding from which this Great End grew in the life of the church. She does not end with history, however, but continues by pointing out with great clarity the relevance of the first Great End to the church's present-day challenges and opportunities. The questions provided at the end of each chapter help readers to reflect further upon Dr. González's thoughts and ponder what they mean for the particular congregations in which they find themselves called to "proclaim the gospel for the salvation of humankind" in word and deed.

This book is the first in a series of six books, one on each of the Great Ends of the Church, that are to be published over the next few years. It is hoped that the series will help Presbyterians rediscover and reclaim the core values that have been part of our rich heritage for hundreds of years and that are still anchor points for our work and witness in the name of Jesus Christ today.

As Dr. González writes, "To be a congregation ready and able to proclaim the gospel for the salvation of humankind is to be the church in its exciting fullness. Proclamation becomes the engine for the renewal of the church that is proclaiming. It renews in the congregation the meaning of the gospel and the experience of salvation. It is a very good place to begin a study of the Great Ends of the Church."

I think you will agree.

**Clifton Kirkpatrick**
**Stated Clerk**
**Presbyterian Church (U.S.A.)**

# Introduction

## The Great Ends of the Church

What do we mean when we speak of the Great Ends of the Church? It would be easy to imagine this as a list of goals the church as a whole should seek to fulfill. There is truth in that understanding. But the term *end* in this case does not mean "goal" exactly. Rather, it means purpose, reason for being. For instance, we can say that the "end" of the family is the protection, nurture and care of its members, especially the creation and formation of the next generation. That does not mean such care is only for some future date. It means that at all times, from the beginning of history, these have been the tasks, the definition, of family. Such ends function as goals in the sense that we are always to carry them out.

We can see the same use of the word *end* in the famous first question of the Westminster Shorter Catechism: "What is the chief end" of human existence? The response, "To glorify God and to enjoy [God] forever," clearly does not mean that we are to do that in the future, but not now. It means, rather, that only by glorifying God are we really fully human, human as God created us to be. In the same way, the Great Ends of the Church are the reasons for its existence, the purposes for which God has called us together. They are marching orders for the present, not goals in the distance toward which we are to strive. Granted, since we do not at present perfectly embody God's purposes for us as the church, the "ends" for which we have been called together also function as targets for the growth and development of the church. They are yardsticks or plumblines by which we measure our current church life.

In a culture dominated by a scientific mentality, we are accustomed to thinking of a cause as that which precedes an effect. We think of cause and effect as the normal sequence: first the cause and then the effect. So when we look for the cause of the church, we look for that which preceded it and led to it historically. Perhaps we think of Jesus actually establishing the church. We look for the cause as coming before that which it effects. But that has not always been the way people thought, nor do we really operate on that basis all the time.

When people decide to go to college they do so at least partly because of the goal they have. The future they desire leads them to make certain decisions. The intended future can be the cause of a present activity. In that case, the "end" or goal determines the present. Events are pulled from the future as well as pushed from the past. The cause of the church is God's desired future, and on that basis God has called the church into being. It is not our past that creates the church but God's future. Since the people of God have existed for millennia in history, the church has a past, and there are causes in that past that have led to effects and continue to do so. But what must determine the church's life is not the past as cause, but the future as "end."

If the Great Ends of the Church represent the purposes or reasons for the church's existence, then when the life of a congregation fails to exhibit these ends in the midst of the social setting in which it lives, the congregation has, to some degree, forfeited its claim to be a church. It has become another human organization, a club, with purposes it has established for itself. To go back to the example of the family: If parents cease to care for their children, if all the members of a biological family stop having any relationship with one another or concern for one another, they have ceased to function as a family. Therefore, to study the Great Ends of the Church, to measure our life as a congregation by these standards, is to see if we are really embodying what it means to be a church.

Notice that we have spoken of the congregation, the local, organized gathering of God's people. It is ultimately at this level that we must measure our life as the church. All the rest exists as support, as connection with other congregations. But the life of the church is judged where the church gathers weekly, where baptisms add to the people of God, where face-to-face meetings are renewed constantly at the Table. We cannot substitute what the church does at the national or presbytery level and assume that this fulfills our obligations. For instance, if the General Assembly or the presbytery has programs of evangelism and mission, and our congregation supports these programs financially, that does not mean we, as a congregation, have become evangelistic. The question is: If Christians form a lived community, how do they exhibit the purposes for which God has called them together? Often they will use the channels of the wider church both as support and as avenues of expression of their concerns. There are very good reasons to carry out international and even national missions at the level of the General Assembly. There are good reasons to have churchwide programs and resources. Yet a congregation's mission does not end when it supports programs at wider levels. The Great Ends of the Church cannot be delegated to other parts of the body of Christ. They are the measure of the faithfulness and genuine "churchness" of each congregation.

Though we are concentrating here on the life of a congregation, we shall see that congregations are not independent units, unconnected to the wider reality of the church. The Ends of the Church are for the whole church, but they are also lived out in the midst of the committed gatherings we call congregations.

Furthermore, these are not specifically "Presbyterian" ends. That is to say, we are not judging in these statements how denominationally oriented a specific congregation is. Rather, the statement of the Great Ends is our understanding of what any church of any denomination ought to be. The structures of a denomination, and the ecumenical relationships it establishes, are for the purpose of helping congregations live out these ends.

The Great Ends of the Church are also not individual. That is, they are not descriptions of what it means to be a Christian. In fact, many of these ends cannot possibly be fulfilled by one person. They are, almost by definition, descriptions of what a community is to be. Granted, these purposes should also give direction to the individual lives of members. The lives of individual members are governed by the fact that they know themselves to be part of the church. Love for others, mercy, and a forgiving and generous spirit all may be virtues an individual can display, but they are only developed and lived in community with others. I may assume I am a loving and forgiving person when I am by myself. It is when I am in community, when I am together with those I find difficult to love or forgive, that I really learn how to develop and exercise these virtues. There is a distinction between the church as a group of interconnected denominational structures, on the one hand, and the personal and interpersonal embodiments of Christian life together on the other.

In the midst of our highly individualistic culture, we are reminded that we are called to be the church, not simply individual Christians. Furthermore, the church is not a gathering of like-minded individuals. Rather, the church is prior to the individual. There would be no Christians without the church. The message of the gospel came to each of us through the proclamation and nurture of a congregation. It is therefore absolutely essential that we examine our common life to make sure we will be able to carry that message to others.

## The Ends Are Plural

The Great Ends of the Church are plural. The text in the Form of Government lists six such ends.

> The Great Ends of the Church are the proclamation of the gospel for the salvation of humankind; the shelter, nurture, and spiritual fellowship of the children of God; the maintenance of divine worship; the preservation of the truth; the promotion of social righteousness; and the exhibition of the Kingdom of Heaven to the world. (*BO*, G-1.0200)[1]

These ends are not listed in order of importance, as though we could choose one or two and ignore the others. All are part of what it means to be the church, and to the degree a congregation fails to exhibit any of them, it fails to be fully the church. This is not because there is a requirement to "pass" an exam as a congregation. Rather, it has to do with the character of the ends themselves.

Think of the six Great Ends as points around a circle, each one related to all the others. That is to say, each of the ends supports the others. Evangelism would be difficult to carry out if the congregation were not nurtured by faithful worship. Nor can worship be faithful if there is no concern for preserving truth. The same connection can be found among all of the ends.

Not only are the six Great Ends connected, they also help define each other. When we speak of the gospel that is proclaimed, that gospel includes and leads to social righteousness, worship, truth, and so forth. One cannot choose one of the ends and let the others be carried out by other congregations.

Since all of the ends are therefore related to all the others, one can enter into a study of this circle at any point, beginning with any one of the ends and progressing through each of the others. The choice of starting points depends on the issues and concerns of the church at the moment. The various confessions in our *Book of Confessions* would place different emphases on the Great Ends. For instance, the Theological Declaration of Barmen stressed the preservation of the truth in the face of Nazi demands concerning the church's teaching:

> In view of the errors of the "German Christians" of the present Reich Church government which are devastating the Church and are also thereby breaking up the unity of the

German Evangelical Church, we confess the following evangelical truths: . . .

Jesus Christ, as he is attested for us in Holy Scripture, is the one Word of God which we have to hear and which we have to trust and obey in life and in death.

We reject the false doctrine, as though the Church could and would have to acknowledge as a source of its proclamation, apart from and besides this one Word of God, still other events and powers, figures and truths, as God's revelation.
(Theological Declaration of Barmen, *BC*, 8.09–.12)

The Confession of 1967, in the midst of the civil rights struggles and other divisions in our nation, stressed reconciliation, which includes "the promotion of social righteousness" and "the exhibition of the Kingdom of Heaven to the world." The Westminster Confession was concerned with the nature of the church as the community of believers, and therefore it stressed "the shelter, nurture, and spiritual fellowship of the children of God," as well as "the maintenance of divine worship." At the same time, we cannot imply that the Westminster Assembly was not also concerned about the preservation of the truth.

The list as we have it shows signs of the origin of the list itself in the early years of the twentieth century, when the Protestant missionary movement was strong. So the first end concerns the evangelistic task of proclaiming the gospel. Evangelism was a strong emphasis in the late nineteenth and early twentieth centuries. It was the great period of Protestant mission efforts around the globe. Evangelism came naturally to the community of faith. There was a renewed realization of the importance of evangelism for the nature of the church itself. Such an emphasis was also supported by the wider culture. Even in secular terms, the nation was sure that its culture, its democratic institutions and values, were to be shared with all the rest of the world. The culture was dominated by Protestant Christian understandings. There was little hesitation to assert that these institutions and values were the best, and needed by all other people.

Today the situation has changed dramatically. Though many congregations are aware of the need for evangelism, we are often confused about what it means or how it can be carried out. We live in the midst of a culture very different from that of the early 1900s. The secular society does not support evangelism, and this makes us question why we should try to have others believe the way we do.

When we read the list of the Great Ends of the Church, we are immediately aware that we are deficient precisely in the area the church in the early twentieth century was most sure about. Therefore it is good for us also to begin by posing the questions about evangelism quite directly. Whereas for them it was a natural starting point because it was a strong element in their life, for us it is a needed starting point because we are weak in this area.

### The First of the Great Ends

The first Great End of the Church is "the proclamation of the gospel for the salvation of humankind." In the following chapters we will look at the meaning and implications of this statement. In chapter 1 we will begin with the meaning of "proclamation." In chapter 2 we will move to the understanding of what the gospel is that is to be proclaimed. Chapter 3 will seek to comprehend what salvation means, both what we are saved from and what we are saved for. Chapter 4 will look at the scope of salvation: for whom is this saving action intended by the proclamation of the gospel?

---

Note
1.  In source references, *BO* stands for the *Book of Order* (Louisville, Ky.: Presbyterian Church (U.S.A.), 2002). *BC* stands for the *Book of Confessions* (Louisville, Ky.: Presbyterian Church (U.S.A.), 2002).

## Study Questions

1. How are the Great Ends of the Church different from goals? How are they the same?

2. Do you see a consistency between the Ends of the Church and your own church's goals as they are listed, for example, in its mission statement?

3. What does González mean by the statement "events are pulled from the future as well as pushed from the past" (p. 2)?

4. What do you think of when you use the word *church*? Do you think that the church universal and the particular church are both legitimate expressions of the meaning?

5. Do you think that the church is necessary for the development of Christian virtues? (See Paul's letter to the Galatians, chap. 5.)

6. It has been noted that the composers of the Great Ends started with the issue they considered most important at the time. With which end would you begin with today?

# 1

# "To Proclaim . . ."

## The Word Itself

The word *proclaim* has a rather archaic sound. We do not use it often in ordinary conversations. Perhaps when young lovers wish to make public their affection, we might say they are proclaiming it. In earlier times kings issued "proclamations." Proclamations are official, authoritative statements. We generally reserve the word *proclaim* for momentous occasions.

The word comes from two roots: *pro*, meaning before, and *clamare*, meaning to cry out. We find this second root in our word *clamor*. By changing the prefix *pro* we alter the word to *acclaim*, or *declaim*, and so forth. To "cry out before" gives us the image of the town crier or the herald, complete with bell or trumpet, calling the attention of the people to the significant public statement that was about to be made.

To proclaim something is more than to announce it. Stores announce sales. Rulers proclaim laws. Couples proclaim their love when they wish it to be known by the whole world. We do not proclaim what is private, if we wish it to remain private. Proclamations are public, statements to the world. The very purpose of proclaiming is to make something public.

There is a risk in proclamation. That is, if the public does not approve of what is being proclaimed, then there can be repercussions. Parents may not approve of the announced love. Even kings knew that their power might be challenged if their proclamations were unpopular.

What this first statement of the Great Ends of the Church declares is that the church exists in order to proclaim. It exists in order to make something public. That cannot be said about all organizations or institutions. For instance, schools exist to educate people. They may wish to announce their programs, they may wish to tell the public what they are about, but they do not exist for the purpose of proclaiming to the world. Families exist for the nurture of their members, particularly for the next generation. Families do not issue proclamations. But the church, as we say in this statement, exists for the purpose of proclaiming something.

## The Problems of Proclaiming Today

In our own day, many of our congregations have a difficult time proclaiming. There are a variety of reasons for this. First, in our culture, we tend to view our relationship to God as something very private. It should not enter into the public sphere of our lives. We need to ask the question, Is our relationship to God indeed a private matter?

In addition, we are not sure to whom we should be proclaiming what we believe. Would it not be better to invite others to come to us, to listen to us if they are interested? We can be welcoming. We can even proclaim our invitation. But to proclaim what we believe seems an invasion of the privacy of others. For this reason, many Presbyterians have difficulties with the whole notion of mission or evangelism.

Furthermore, we are not sure exactly what it is we should proclaim. Is it something about our own experience? Is it something objective that is other than ourselves? Is it something about what our congregation is like? Is it announcing services we provide to the community? Finally, even if we agree we should proclaim something; even if we agree about what it is we should proclaim; how do we do it in this culture? Do we put advertisements in the paper? Buy time on radio or television? Stand on the street corner? All of these questions are in our minds when we hear the statement: the church exists for the purpose of proclaiming. Let us look at some of these problems.

### Public versus Private Realms

For several centuries, Western culture has made an increasingly clear division between what belongs to the private realm and what to the public. What can be demonstrated scientifically, objectively, regardless of personal biases and opinions, can be discussed publicly. This has been the ideal of truth since the modern period began in the seventeenth and eighteenth centuries. Other matters, such as religious beliefs, are viewed as personal opinions. Each person has a right to his or her own, and there is no expectation that such beliefs need to be proven in any rigorous, scientific way. In fact, there is the sense that they could not be. Religious beliefs are therefore "opinions," not "facts."

This may sound rather condescending toward religion; and in fact, it is. The question of how faith can properly address public issues is a major concern in our society today. We will come back to this issue later. However, although it is clear that this disjunction between public truth and private truth came about because of new standards of truth based on developments in science, it was accepted by societies in general for some other reasons as well.

In the seventeenth century, Europe had been racked by wars of religion in the aftermath of the Protestant Reformation. It was a bloody and destructive time. Even though religion was used as a cloak for political power, it was clear to many people that a secular state was a great advantage over a state that enforced a particular religion on all people. We can see the wisdom of such toleration even in our own day, when we see ethnic conflicts around the globe that pit Protestant against Catholic in Ireland, Muslim against Orthodox against Catholic in the Balkans, Muslim against Christian in Indonesia, Hindu against Muslim on the Indian subcontinent, and Islamist, Christian, and Jewish fundamentalists against religious groups with whom they disagree.

A secular state that permits people to choose their own religion and practice has great advantages over state religion. But the result is the privatizing of religion, which raises the question of how public one can make one's private opinions. Are we invading the "private space" of another person when we ask about their faith or tell them about ours? Our culture makes us think twice about doing either. To speak publicly about our faith—to proclaim it—puts it in the arena of public truth and takes it out of the realm of private opinion. It asserts that our religious view is a fact, something true for all people, not just for us. That is a difficult assertion to make after several centuries of thinking otherwise. It is not only that we hesitate to speak to others about our Christian faith. We may also be somewhat embarrassed if someone asks us about our faith. It is as though they had asked about something too personal to discuss. In addition, in this country we assume there should be a great deal of personal freedom to choose what to believe or do, as long as such actions do not infringe on the freedom of others. There is outcry against laws about personal safety—wearing seat belts or helmets, for instance—as though this were an invasion of personal freedom. What we do is no one else's business. If we wish to take risks, that is our concern. The thought that our actions do affect others, whether in higher insurance costs because our freedom leads to injury that results in large medical bills, or whether our actions lead young people to follow our example, is disregarded.

All of these factors together mean that for many inside and outside the church, religious truth is truth for me. It is not necessarily truth for anyone else. Their truth in religious matters may be quite different than mine, and I am bound to respect that. Under the proper circumstances, I might tell someone else about my experience of God, but my truth may not speak to them, and we must leave it at that. Scientific truth, objective truth, may be pushed as universal. Religious truth is by this definition subjective and ought not to be considered universal. Such a climate obviously makes evangelism difficult.

## The Authority of the Church

Underlying many of our questions is the issue of authority. We live in a highly individualistic culture. We assume that people have a right to their own beliefs, and that others should not infringe on this right. Nor should an institution speaking in their name limit this right, even if they are members of it. For the church to issue a proclamation seems to allow the church an authority it should not have.

We have seen this attitude in our denomination when the General Assembly has spoken on behalf of the whole church, and many individual Presbyterians have been annoyed that the Assembly thought it could speak for all Presbyterians. A proclamation by the church, be it congregation or General Assembly, seems to give to the institution more authority than many in our culture wish to give it. This is not only an issue for Presbyterians. Even churches that have been accustomed to having great authority in the lives of their members, such as the Roman Catholic Church, are finding the same response from many of their members in this country.

The issue of authority is even more complex for the church than for other institutions in our society. When the church proclaims, on whose behalf is it speaking? In one sense, it is announcing to the world what its members believe. In another sense, however, it is declaring God's word to the world. What is the connection between these two? That is part of the difficulty. For whom is the church speaking when it proclaims? For its members? For God? For both?

We have lost much of the sense of the church as a divine as well as a human organization. Again, in part this is due to the scientific worldview or mentality within which we live. We analyze institutions sociologically, politically, economically, and so on. When we do, we can look at the church in the same way we would look at any other organization in our society. That is the only way the social sciences can proceed. We do with the church what we also do with the Bible when we deal with it as we would any other piece of historical literature. This does not mean that science is evil. But it does mean that it is limited in the conclusions it can reach. The social sciences can and should deal with the church as a human organization. That is to be expected. We also, as members of the church, need to remember that the church is indeed a human institution and prone to all the frailties of any human endeavor. The social sciences can aid us in this awareness.

For believers, however, the church must be more than a human institution. It is not a human creation. It is the creation of God in Christ. It is the body of Christ. It is a divine creation just as much as it is a human institution. Human science can and should only study the human character of the church. Believers, however, ought to know the divine mystery that is also the church.

When believers are so embedded in the scientifically oriented culture in which we live that they forget this divine dimension of the reality of the church, then they too act as though it is only a human institution. It speaks for its members, and it has no right to speak for us when we do not give it permission to do so.

We see this issue arise in many aspects of the church's life. For instance, let us look at questions about the Form of Government. It has been part of the historic understanding of Presbyterians that no "instructed delegates" can be elected to any governing body. That is to say, congregational members cannot elect elders on the basis of how they promise they will vote on issues. Presbyteries cannot quiz potential commissioners to General Assembly as to how they will vote on questions coming before that body, and then elect them only if they agree to vote in a certain way. Governing bodies must be free to listen to God's voice when they deliberate. They are to be open to the movement of the Holy Spirit in their decisions. Therefore, they cannot be instructed beforehand. (See the Form of Government, *BO*, G-4.0300d.)

Today, however, there is often a desire to alter this arrangement. If governing bodies are to "represent" us, then they should vote the way we would. That is the human understanding. The church is more than a human institution, but only to the degree that it is open to the leading of God. Does God act in the church when it makes decisions? Ought we as a congregation to elect as elders those who agree most with our opinions or those who seem most able to listen to God? This may be a difficult distinction to make if we assume our opinion is the only one God agrees with. To elect uninstructed delegates is to give to governing bodies more authority than many of us are comfortable with, when we view the church only as a human organization.

On the other hand, if those who are elected do not actually seek the guidance of God but rather treat their office as a position of power in a secular fashion, then those who elect them are even more likely to want to see the political "platform" upon which they seek to be elected, before the vote takes place. Faithfulness on the part of the members in choosing officers as well as faithfulness on the part of those who are elected are the only guarantees that our system of church government actually will work. To deal with the church as only a human institution is to corrupt the system.

No system of church government can function properly without faithfulness. Probably every system will work if its members and officers are truly seeking to be faithful. What Presbyterians have devised is a system of government that limits the damage a few unfaithful people can do by curtailing severely the power any one person has. But it is no guarantor in itself that it will work well. Where does the power lie for encouraging faithfulness in the whole system? Ultimately with congregations. If they elect as their elders those who exhibit a desire and an ability to seek God's will for their life and the life of the church, and if congregations elect as pastors those who seek to develop this ability within themselves and the congregation, the system will work ultimately. Without these building blocks, nothing will work as it should.

## Confusion about What We Are Selling

Many of the television evangelists make it appear that the church is selling God. We recoil at such an approach. God is not a commodity that can be advertised as useful. We know that. There is clear witness in scripture that those who are faithful may find their lives disrupted and the price of discipleship high. God makes demands. Many Presbyterians therefore are reluctant, and rightly so, to say that faithfulness to God will make our lives better in purely secular terms.

We have had little hesitation, however, about selling the church and equating that with evangelism. If we are comfortable proclaiming anything to do with Christianity, it is probably about our congregation. We are friendly, have a great music program, a great preacher, a youth program, a mission program, whatever it is that we think will bring in new members. We even develop programs so that the congregation will be more appealing to outsiders. We are selling the services the church provides. We seek to make the church useful to the community. Obviously, some of this is good. The congregation needs to be about mission in the world. But proclamation about what the church can do for you is not the same as proclamation about what God has done for us.

Perhaps our reluctance to speak about God's action and our eagerness to speak about our congregation goes back to the previous discussion about the scientific mentality within which we live. What God has done for us is not a public fact. It is a private opinion in this understanding. What a particular congregation offers in its programs is, however, a sociological reality. It can be shown, documented, proved for all who enter into its life. For a congregation that is uncomfortable discussing the life of faith, the cost of discipleship, or the demands of the gospel, speaking about the programs the church offers can be a great relief. But is it false advertising?

Presbyterians are accustomed to having a well-educated, socially involved, and relatively influential membership. Precisely because of these characteristics, we have been greatly affected by the scientific mentality around us. We have been a part of it and even nurtured it. This is generally true of all the denominations we term "mainline." As congregations, we usually appeal to others of the same mindset. But programs are not the same as proclamation. We are often very good at programs and very poor at proclamation. We can show others our congregation. We cannot show others God or our faith in any similarly objective fashion. We can advertise our congregation, but that is not the same as proclamation.

Others may well come for all the reasons we have given them. But when they do come, will we ever be able to speak of God? of faith? of discipleship? Or will our inability to speak continue, even within the life of the church itself? When we do speak of God, do we do so with the attitude that "of course, this is only my opinion, my experience, and it may have nothing to do with anyone else"? Or do we proclaim? As a congregation, do we proclaim? And how will we proclaim anything about God and the life of faith if we are unable to speak about these matters in the congregation?

## The Authority of Scripture

Were we to speak, by what authority would we say whatever we said? Would it be our own experience? For Presbyterians, the usual answer to the question of by what authority we speak is, by authority of the Scriptures. Here at last there is an objective authority that we can look at. We can point to verses and claim God's word. But it is not so simple. We are well aware of the conflicts between scientific understandings of the world and the passages in Genesis about creation. Debates about evolution continue. Is Genesis "science"? Is evolution as much a personal opinion as creationism? What should be taught in schools? Such debates, particularly in the early decades of the twentieth century, increased the sense that religion ought to be kept out of the public arena, where only the universal truths determined by science ought to have a voice.

In addition to the debates about science and religion, the question of how we are to interpret Scripture has divided our church. Generally, there have been two opinions. Stated in extreme form, one holds that the Bible contains the word of God in such a fashion that all those who read it can discover the truth. It is objective. The Bible creates faith, it does not require faith in order to be understood. The other opinion holds that the Holy Spirit must act within the individual reading the Bible in order for it to be real revelation. It is in this sense subjective. Faith is therefore the work of the Holy Spirit, not of the printed text of the Scriptures. All the reading in the world will not make the Bible revelatory if the Holy Spirit is not at work in us, both individually and corporately. Surely the truth lies somewhere between these extreme positions, but we as a church have had a difficult time in the midst of a scientifically oriented culture to have the Bible function well as authority.

Furthermore, in our own generation, we have become aware of the subjective character of all biblical interpretation. However infallible the text may be, when we apply it to situations today, we are interpreting it. Interpretations are not infallible. They are affected by our cultural assumptions, by our church traditions, and a variety of other factors. When these are not acknowledged, they can corrupt our interpretations. What is obvious to one church member is not at all obvious to another who reads the same text. Interpretation is therefore seen as personal opinion, and one person's opinion is seen as no more valid than another's. In this situation, the Bible has little authority to adjudicate opinions.

Finally, however well various forms of biblical interpretation worked in the past, they all assumed a general knowledge of Scripture. Such knowledge can no longer be presupposed. There is enormous biblical illiteracy in our congregations. The Bible may be viewed as having authority, theoretically, but if it is not read and studied, it has no functional authority in our lives. We may cling to one verse that supports our opinion, but as a congregation, we may find that Scripture does not really function as an authority.

## Signs of Hope

Thus far we have painted a rather dismal picture of the current life of the church. But that is not totally true to the reality. There are many signs of hope and renewal. These are events within the wider society and in congregations that are responding to the issues raised above.

## Changes in the Culture

One reason for hope is that, culturally, we have taken the divide between public and private spheres of life to such extremes that obviously something needs to change. For instance, can any values be taught in the public schools, or are schools only to teach "facts"? Is honesty simply a personal opinion or something that can be publicly demanded in students? Is responsibility just some people's private value or something that can be defined and required in school?

We are beginning to have serious questions also about the individualism that has been so pervasive. How do we balance individual rights against the good of society? Are there limits to free speech when it involves intimidation of others? From zoning issues, to smoking and gun control, from censorship on the Internet, to ratings of television shows and movies, we are in the midst of constant discussion and battles about the individualism that has been with us since our nation was born.

It is important to realize that, whereas other societies had long histories of social traditions before the modern worldviews developed, our society was formed at the same time as a scientific perspective and the individualism of industrialism came into being. We have no "before" as a culture. Furthermore, individualism was increased by the movement to the frontier and by the patterns of immigration. Those who left the older cultures voluntarily in order to come here left behind the social institutions that put the wider society ahead of the individual. Both the frontier and immigration increased individualism. The fact that immigrants from the very beginning of our history represented so many different religious traditions increased the move toward separation of church and state, led to the rejection of the idea of a state church, and therefore increased the push to make religious views part of a private rather than a public sphere. Precisely because of our history, we have been more extreme in regard to the division between private and public truth, and in our stress on the individual, than older societies have been. We are now at the beginning of serious questions about these issues. As the church, we need to be part of this discussion. As congregations, we need to understand how these issues affect our task of proclamation.

## The Quest for Spirituality and Biblical Literacy

Spirituality is not a term Presbyterians would have used a generation ago. In fact, we might have assumed it had something to do with "spiritualism," which means communicating with the dead by means of crystal balls or ouija boards. But now there are many nonbiblical forms of spirituality, many of which are private and personal or constructed from Eastern religions. Even in the Christian tradition, both within our denomination and within others, there are hundreds of books on spirituality, study groups on devotional literature, classes on the life of prayer, and prayer groups in congregations, all growing rapidly. Pastors and laypeople alike are developing skills in leading such groups.

Though there can be an extreme individualism in some forms of spirituality, as if I could develop my own spiritual life and not need the community of faith at all, this is much truer of New Age forms. Much of the current trend within Christianity leads in a different direction: to a renewal of congregational life. It makes people comfortable speaking with others about their own life of faith. Such renewal in the life of a congregation is not in itself proclamation, but it is a necessary preliminary if there is to be any proclamation at all. If we are not sure what faith means in our own lives, or if we cannot discuss such matters within the congregation, we can hardly be expected to say anything very clearly to the world at large.

The Form of Government, recognizing that this is the situation in many of our congregations, makes it clear that the session is called "to provide opportunities for evangelism to be learned and practiced in and by the church, that members may be better equipped to articulate their faith, to witness in word and deed to the saving grace of Jesus Christ, and to invite persons into a new life in Christ, in accordance with G-3.0300" (*BO*, G-10.0102).

Similarly, in many of our congregations there is a hunger for knowledge of the Bible. Biblical illiteracy is so pervasive that members no longer feel self-conscious in acknowledging it. There are demands for courses, many of which require significant time commitment. Where such study exists, especially where it is not individual but in groups, the Bible begins to claim its authority in the lives of church members.

In the case of the small groups gathered for growth in their spiritual lives and those gathered for Bible study, there is an added dimension. Many of these studies are part of national programs. There are training sessions, there is published material. There are also short-term classes available at seminaries and colleges for both clergy and laity. Both clergy and laity lead study groups in congregations. Laypeople who have undergone significant renewal in their own lives of faith are becoming leaders in the congregation. That means that there is a greater pool of committed people from which a congregation can elect officers. This will eventually affect the whole life of the denomination and the wider church. This is indeed a great sign of hope for the future.

Furthermore, where there are such groups—people within a congregation who actually speak to each other about their faith—the barrier between private and public truth begins to be overcome. Here we see the connection between various Great Ends of the Church. The development of such groups, the cultivation of the spiritual life of a congregation, is in itself not part of the task of proclamation. However, unless such spirituality is encouraged within our congregations, there can be no authentic proclamation. The nurture of Bible study leads to the experience of the authority of Scripture. This in turn supports the ends of "preserving the truth" and "the promotion of social righteousness."

## To Whom Are We Proclaiming?

We often speak of that portion of the Sunday worship service that includes the reading of Scripture and the sermon as "the proclamation of the word." The church needs to hear the proclamation of the gospel in order to be renewed and strengthened in its faith. That is part of the nurture of the people of God. We gather to hear the proclamation for our own sake, as creatures who so readily forget or change the gospel. It is not only in the sermon that the Word is proclaimed. When Paul reminds the Corinthian church of the institution of the Lord's Supper, he writes that "as often as you eat this bread and drink the cup, you proclaim the Lord's death until he comes" (1 Cor. 11:26). Remember, that when these words were written, only baptized Christians would have been present at the Communion service. Therefore, Paul cannot mean that the wider, non-Christian public is somehow seeing the proclamation of the gospel through seeing Christians gathered at the Table.

To whom is the sacrament proclaiming? We cannot say we are proclaiming to ourselves, gathered together, for the text says that we are the ones proclaiming. Many early Christians—like many still in the Eastern church—believed that Christians who gathered at the Lord's Table were proclaiming to the "principalities and powers," to the power of evil that thinks it controls this world, that through the victory of Christ in the resurrection, the kingdom of God has indeed begun. We shall deal with this more in the next chapter. But it needs to be said that the church proclaims the gospel, not only to the world around it, but also to the powers we cannot see that corrupt our common human life.

Though the church always needs to hear the gospel, there is a sense in which proclamation is by definition public. It is the public telling of what God has done for us. Therefore, proclamation is not primarily an in-house activity of the church. We do not proclaim mainly for those already part of the church. We proclaim for those who are not yet part of the community of faith. The church nurtures those who are already part of its life. It proclaims to those who are not.

Proclamation is related to evangelism, though it is not exactly the same. That is to say, proclamation is the public statement. It is done for the purpose of giving those who do not know it the good news the church has to tell. For many Presbyterians, the term *evangelism* is less appealing than proclamation. It seems to involve convincing, arguing, even threatening others. Evangelism, it would appear, means trying to convert others. Much of this attitude comes from some traditions of evangelism that we do not like. They do seem an intrusion into the lives of others. Presbyterians have been clear that only God can convert others. It is beyond our power. It is the work of the Holy Spirit. Yet Presbyterians have also known that the Spirit usually works by opening the eyes and ears of others to respond to the message of the gospel. Therefore, the proclamation of the gospel lays the groundwork for the work of the Spirit. As a church, we have often been so uncomfortable about some forms of evangelism that we have failed to do the basic task of proclamation.

Because so many church members hesitate to speak about their faith, there is a tendency to substitute invitations to come to church for proclamation. Of course there must be such invitations. But when they are the only form of proclamation that exists, what effect does it have on the rest of the church's life? It means we anticipate that those who accept our invitation and join us in worship will hear proclamation there. But if proclamation is evangelism, does that mean that faithful church members and interested but uncommitted neighbors are being treated alike? Are members starting at the beginning every Sunday, as though their baptism meant nothing? Are they being considered potential disciples but not already faithful? Or does the service assume that the uncommitted have faith, no matter whether they do or not, which also implies that baptism is unnecessary. Doing our evangelism in our Sunday morning worship is a serious issue. It can weaken rather than strengthen the church.

Many of our battles about the style and content of worship derive from this. The proliferation of "seekers services" is an attempt to divide the services for those who are uncommitted from the services for those already members of the congregation. But is there evidence that the seekers do actually graduate from this form of worship and join with the rest of the congregation? There is no easy answer, but understanding that proclamation cannot be confined to the church building, with invitations issued to come and hear the gospel, can lead to asking the basic questions about evangelism. It can also lead to asking the basic questions about both worship and nurture. Many churches, especially those in cultures that are not traditionally Christian, have a lengthy program for those who are interested in the church, but not yet ready for membership. This may include participation in worship, but it also incorporates a variety of other events designed particularly for seekers. Because we live in a culture that assumed almost everyone was a Christian, we have not felt we needed much of any preparation for church membership. That is changing now. Because the society is increasingly secular, we can no longer count on a general knowledge of Christianity in the wider society. Presbyterian congregations that had never had an adult baptism until recently have had several in the past few years. This is an increasing trend. We need to develop programs for preparation for church membership for those who have not been nurtured by the church during childhood and young adulthood. They are truly converts, and not Christians moving from one congregation— or denomination—to another.

Proclamation must occur in the public arena. For a congregation, the public is the wider community within which the congregation lives its life. There are two inhibitions that congregations face. The first has already been discussed: the cultural assumption that religion is a private matter, highly personal, and should not enter into public life. The second is the constitutional issue of separation of church and state, and how this plays out in terms of the church's role in the society. Because churches are not-for-profit, tax-exempt institutions, they cannot be political. One may question whether this status is healthy for the church, but that is the current situation. Therefore, the church can speak out on issues that face the community, it can do so in the name of the congregation, but it cannot be politically involved.

We have a long history of division in our church between those who are committed to social action and those who wish to stress the personal life of faith. There will be no answer to the question of how we can proclaim our faith in the public arena until we heal this division within our own church life. There are signs it is healing. Those who are committed to social justice discover burnout is rapid if their commitment is not nurtured by a constantly growing life of faith, supported by a community. Part of the reason for this burnout is that success is measured differently by faith than by secular activism. We are astonished at the lives of people like Mother Teresa of Calcutta and her order. How can such people keep doing what they are doing? Are they successful? How would you measure it? There are still the poor dying alone. They have not solved that problem. But they are serving their neighbors; they are making a public proclamation of their faith; they are growing in their love for others. Such actions do not preclude seeking to alter structures of society that create such problems. But we cannot stand on the sidelines and issue orders to government without being intimately involved in responding to the need we see. Nor can we stay involved very long, undiscouraged, without a vibrant faith.

What are the issues our communities will face in the coming years? Latchkey children, availability of medical services, improving education, nursing homes and care for the elderly, teenage mothers, illiteracy, refugees, parenting skills, strengthening marriages, ethnic and racial conflicts, alcoholism, drugs, landfills, prisons, juvenile justice, water and air quality. The list is endless. How is our faith related to these issues? What do we believe that impacts these concerns? What can we say to the wider community? What can we do that shows our faith in action? What can we say that shows why we are doing what we are doing? How are these local issues related to national or global ones? How can our involvement in a connectional church—with governing bodies at all levels—help raise this issue to a wider level? What are the local ramifications of issues the national church is already dealing with?

What does this mean in practice? Could a congregation make a community aware of a problem that needs to be addressed? Could it begin responding to the need it has discovered? Could it indicate on the basis of its faith why this need must be addressed? Could it call upon others to join in finding solutions? Could it form coalitions to have the political institutions play their role? Congregations have often found it easier to take stands on foreign policy issues than on problems at their own doorstep. Yet their proclamation—based on their faith—could have much greater impact if it were local. We cannot separate local and global issues, but we can find local ways to address global issues.

What can a congregation do? It can network with others in the area —other faith-based communities as well as secular ones. It can provide space for discussion, space for some of the solutions such as food banks or after-school programs. Obviously, many congregations are doing this. But is it seen as part of the congregation's proclamation? Proclamation takes words as well as actions. Is the community clear about the whys of our actions?

Proclamation is words. Our hesitation to speak about our faith often leads us to act without saying why. We console ourselves with the thought that actions speak louder than words. The church exists in order to proclaim, however, and we cannot be silent. Our fear of stepping out of the private and into the public with our words as well as our actions makes our proclamation weak. If greater attention to prayer and Bible study within the congregation leads a group to get involved in meeting a need in the community; if the congregation supports them in this; if they can communicate to the public why, on the basis of the gospel, they are led to do what they are doing, proclamation will take place in the public sphere.

## Called to Be Witnesses

There are several passages in the latter portion of the book of Isaiah that describe very clearly the task of proclamation by the people of God. The situation is the experience of exile in Babylon after the destruction of Jerusalem. The prophet writes:

> Do not fear, or be afraid;
>> have I not told you from of old and declared it?
> You are my witnesses!

*(Isa. 44:8)*

> Thus says the LORD, your Redeemer, the Holy One of Israel:
> I am the LORD your God,
>> who teaches you for your own good,
>> who leads you in the way you should go.
> O that you had paid attention to my commandments!
>> Then your prosperity would have been like a river,
>> and your success like the waves of the sea;
> your offspring would have been like the sand,
>> and your descendants like its grains;
>> their name would never be cut off or destroyed from
>>> before me.
> Go out from Babylon, flee from Chaldea,
>> declare this with a shout of joy, proclaim it,
> send it forth to the end of the earth;
> say, "The LORD has redeemed his servant Jacob!"

*(Isa. 48:17–20)*

In the New Testament, especially in the book of Acts, the followers of Jesus are called to be his witnesses. Israel and the church are alike in their task of witnessing. They are chosen for that purpose.

Witnesses proclaim what they know. They make official, public statements about their knowledge. The people of God are chosen for the task of proclamation because they are firsthand witnesses of God's actions. They are witnesses, not to themselves, but to the unbelieving world in which they live. Nor are they witnessing in a comfortable, supportive situation. Israel was in exile, having been conquered by the Babylonians. The early Christian disciples were living under the Roman Empire that did not permit new religions.

The actions mentioned in Isaiah 48 are twofold. First, God teaches us what is good, what truly leads to a good life, not only for individuals, but for society. In fact, it is not possible for an individual to have a good life, a life of satisfying relationships, work, and leisure, if the society does not have such a life. These directions for a good life are what the Bible calls the law. The law is part of the gracious action of God to teach the people so that they can live happily together.

Second, God redeems us. The word about redemption is what we call the gospel. Our proclamation needs to take both of these elements —the law and the gospel—into account. In both cases, we are witnesses to what God has done.

The Bible is our source for knowing the history of what God has done. However, we are not simply reporting what we have read. We are witnesses proclaiming that we know that what is written is true because we have experienced its reality in our own lives. In a later chapter we shall deal more fully with what redemption or salvation means to Christians. Here we will look at the issue of the knowledge of the way we should live that is also to be part of our proclamation.

## Pious Living

### The Grace of the Law

In common understanding today, the law represents authority, bound-aries, limits, restrictions, lack of freedom. It is therefore negative. That is often the way we view it. The law is filled with things we should not do. That also sounds negative. In Christian history, the law has sometimes been presented as that which condemns us, as that which shows us how sinful we are. Its opposite is grace, which is a gift, brings forgiveness, and therefore is positive. Grace is generous and not demanding, whereas law is judgmental and unforgiving. That, however, is much too sharp a distinction, nor is it the understanding we find here in Isaiah. Neither our reading of Scripture nor our own experience leads us to believe that law and gospel are opposites.

The law is a gracious gift of God. It describes what we as human beings were created to be. In that sense, the law is the "manufacturer's instructions" that show how human society was intended to work. If we do not live in this fashion, our society does not work the way it was created to work. In the same way that those who try to put together or operate something without reading the instructions are likely to end up with parts not working, so those who try to live without going by the instructions are likely to create a malfunctioning society.

The law is not individual. It is a law for society. It tells us how we are to understand ourselves as human beings, and how we are to live together, to treat each other. If a whole society follows the law, then the society will work well. If it does not, then there will be disaster, even if a few individuals within it are really trying. In fact, the ones trying to live by the law may suffer persecution because of their witness. The law is, by its very nature, social. Fulfilling the law is its own reward for a society, and failing to live by it brings its own negative consequences.

The people of God are to witness to the law, not to scare people into repentance so that individually they will earn salvation after they die, but to witness to the world what needs to be done in order to be a good society, a well-functioning society that leads to a good life for all its members. God's people have a witness to make to the world about what is necessary for such a society. This is God's world, created to be good and work well. That is a witness that must be made in the public arena because that is where it must be enacted.

We are to witness, not to force, even if we had the political power to do so. The hard-won toleration that prevents a church from imposing its beliefs on all citizens must remain. Theocracies do not have a very good record on creating healthy societies. However, the witness of the church can lead to alliances with others outside the community of faith who realize the rightness of the church's position on specific issues. The greatest witness the church can make is not simply to speak but so to live by the law that others are persuaded.

The law is therefore to be proclaimed as positive, not negative. Though such a view runs counter to the understanding that is prevalent in our society, it is true to Christian experience. We see it most clearly in the lives of those who have lived outside the law, who have lived obviously sinful and antisocial lives. If they go through a serious conversion experience, their witness is that the law they once abhorred is indeed good, and part of their conversion experience is to begin living in accordance with the law. They see it now as a joyful way of life. As parents, it is our hope for our children that they will grow past an adolescent rebellion against law into a mature acceptance of its guidance. We can hope no less for society as a whole.

**How Shall We Witness?**

The public around us needs to know more about who we are than just the fact that we are a friendly congregation that invites them to attend and use its services. There is a difference between pressuring people to join the church and proclaiming who we are as the church. It is for this reason that we need to give reasons for our actions in the world. The church is also more than a group that has some insight on how to live satisfying lives, important as the law may be. Ultimately the witness of the church is that we are those whom God has redeemed through the work of Christ and, therefore, our lives have been transformed. We are inviting them to participate in such transformation. That is the proclamation of the gospel.

The focus of proclamation is not who we are, or even who we have become. It is who God is, and what God has done and is doing. If church members are comfortable speaking this language to each other, if they overcome their hesitancy to speak it in public, if they can proclaim the law as a gracious gift of God to the world, and if they are able to base their mission as a congregation on the gospel message, then their witness and their proclamation will be clear.

We must now turn to the content of the gospel we are called upon to proclaim.

# Study Questions

1. What kinds of things does one proclaim? What are some challenges characterizing the act of proclamation that someone publicizing a proven fact, for example, would not be likely to encounter?

2. Do you think that our relationship to God is "a private matter"? In what ways might it be private and in what ways public?

3. What is the value of the separation of church and state? In what ways is our faith both objective, based on a truth that is public, involving more than ourselves as individuals, and subjective, or private? How do you think the balance between these dynamics is best maintained?

4. Freedom is an important American value. Many believe that we can do what we want as long as our actions do not negatively affect someone else, and that we have no obligations to others beyond doing no harm. How does freedom characterize our lives as Christians?

5. The government of the Presbyterian Church has been designed to maintain a certain kind of freedom that "balances" the dynamics of power between the individual conscience and a communal understanding of the gospel. How do you see this functioning in your own church? At the level of your presbytery? At the level of the General Assembly?

6. What does González mean when she says that the church has both a human and a divine dimension? What does she lift up as the unique power of congregations?

7. Do you feel comfortable proclaiming the grace of the gospel? Have you felt the unease the author describes when you have proclaimed the gospel to people outside your congregation? Within your congregation or denomination? What makes these different for you?

8. What authority does Scripture hold in your life? How is it different within your congregational life and in your workplace, for instance? How do you or your congregation understand the struggle between the authority of Scripture and that of science?

9. González says that the Bible can have theoretical authority, but unless it is read and studied, it can be void of functional authority. Do you agree with this statement?

10. Valuing is a personal action, but determining factual truth is more objective and communally applicable. How do you think that the bridge between value, which grounds religious truth, and facts, which ground rules and laws, can be strengthened? How can both individual and group rights and integrity be maintained?

11. The proclamation of the gospel is a task to which we are called as a church. It is not optional. At the same time, in North America both individualism and religious diversity challenge this task in different ways. González attributes this partially to a more strict separation between church and state than has been characteristic of other cultures. Recently, many national events have brought the United States to a new awareness of our relationship to other cultures and religions in which we are less isolated from the rest of the world than we had thought. How do you think that this increasing sense of diverse cultural and religious values affects our proclamation?

12. The authority of Scripture is not automatic but discovered among believers as they study the Bible together. Why do you think that

Scripture's authority may be less clear to individuals who study it alone? Why does González say that unless individuals within a congregation speak to one another about their faith and engage in Bible study together, "there can be no authentic proclamation"?

13. Is proclamation the same thing as evangelism? How is it different? In what ways is proclamation nurture? Why is the division between social action and the personal life of faith an issue for González? Do you feel this pull or tension?

14. How can proclamation also be action? What is the challenge when proclamation takes this form?

# 2

# The Gospel

The first Great End of the Church is the proclamation of the gospel, so it is essential that we have a very clear understanding of what the gospel is. We may assume that since we are Christians, we understand the gospel and have no need for further clarification. But the history of the church shows the constant need for such reexamination. Throughout the twenty centuries of the church's existence, Christians have been tempted to limit the scope of the gospel to that which is readily compatible with their own culture. This is quite understandable. It is very difficult to be aware of our own assumptions. They are like the air we breathe. We assume that the way we understand things is obviously the way they are. When something totally new is suggested, something that completely goes against our understanding of the world, we either reject it out of hand as absurd, or we fit it into our existing view of reality and therefore lose the newness.

When the gospel is first proclaimed in a culture it may seem so new as to be unbelievable. For some, it is astonishing good news, and they join the church. Others simply declare it ridiculous. But when the church becomes part of a culture, the message it proclaims often has been sufficiently tailored so that it is quite believable within that culture. Therefore some of the original meaning and the newness has been lost. When the gospel becomes readily believable, quite compatible with the rest of the culture, then it is no longer news. Our understanding of the gospel may therefore be limited and need to be expanded.

At the same time, it must also be said that the gospel is always proclaimed in a culture. Ultimately, it must reflect that culture and not be totally alien to it. There is legitimate acculturation that needs to go on as a people of a specific culture live out the significance of the gospel in the midst of their own society. The gospel is not something that remains alien to the receiving culture. This means that there are always variations in the way the good news is understood. That has been true from the earliest days. The Gospel according to Matthew and the Gospel according to John are not the same. Paul's letters are not the same as John's letters. The book of Revelation is not like Hebrews. The social situation and the culture of both the writer and the original readers shapes the writings. Yet all proclaim the one gospel. Such variations have been seen throughout the history of the church, and still remain. The difficulty is knowing what is legitimate acculturation and what is limiting the gospel to what is already believed in the culture, therefore rendering the gospel bland and not news.

In chapter 1 we saw how the culture in which we live assumes that only scientifically proven matters can really be objective and so deserve to be public, and how other matters, such as taste in movies, literature, lifestyles, including religious beliefs, are personal choices, and so should be left to individual tastes. They need no scientific proof, nor could they have any. By definition, then, we assume our personal choices should not be imposed on the public at large.

The term *gospel* means "the good news." However, if the gospel is made a matter of optional lifestyle that is quite private, then it is not understood to be news for the world at large. On the other hand, if the gospel is made compatible with what the wider culture already believes so that it already is public, then nothing really new to the culture is proclaimed.

Sometimes the way the church has proclaimed its message makes it appear more bad news than good news. That has happened when the church has said: "Agree with us or you will suffer forever." The gospel then seems more threatening and condemning than a positive invitation. To keep the gospel both "news" and "good" is not an easy matter. Yet it is a task that must be done. It requires faithfulness and constant vigilance. If we have no news, proclamation is impossible. If we have no good news, that which really would make a joyful difference in the lives of our neighbors, then we have no positive basis for evangelism. Our understanding of the gospel message is the central factor in our ability to evangelize.

What was this good news the early church felt driven to proclaim? We begin with the very simplest statement.

## Jesus Is Lord

The earliest content of the gospel probably was the brief statement "Jesus is Lord." It does not say Jesus is my lord, as though there were others I might have chosen. The statement says Jesus is the lord of all, the only ultimate lord there is, the lord of those who acknowledge him and the lord of those who do not. It was a statement about objective reality.

This declaration or proclamation goes against our hesitancy to declare anything objectively true that cannot be scientifically established. It is also an affront to contemporary views about the subjectivity of all religious beliefs. For instance, we often speak about those who make money or fame or power into a god. In one sense it is saying something very true: that such lives are centered on the goal that they have chosen, and therefore they have no room in their lives for the true God.

In another sense, such statements are misleading. However we live our lives, it does not change the objective reality that money or fame or power are not the ultimate rulers of creation. Whatever we believe, whatever is the ruling principle of our lives, is subjectively true about us, but not true about reality itself. We do not have the power to create God. We can only create idols. That is the message of the great Hebrew prophets.

Look at the satire on idols and their worshipers that is found in Isaiah 44:9–20 and 46:1–13. If we worship the true God, it is not because we have elevated God to this position but because we have encountered One who has laid claim to our lives. It is this God who has called us to be witnesses. We read in Isaiah:

Bel bows down, Nebo stoops,

    their idols are on beasts and cattle;

these things you carry are loaded as burdens

    on weary animals. . . .

Listen to me, O house of Jacob,

    all the remnant of the house of Israel,

who have been borne by me from your birth,

    carried from the womb;

Even to your old age I am [God],

    even when you turn gray I will carry you.

I have made, and I will bear;

I will carry and will save.

*(Isa. 46:1; 3–4)*

Look also at what Habakkuk says:

> What use is an idol
>> once its maker has shaped it—
>> a cast image, a teacher of lies?
>
> For its maker trusts in what has been made,
>> though the product is only an idol
>> that cannot speak!
>
> Alas for you who say to the wood, "Wake up!"
>> to silent stone, "Rouse yourself!"
>> Can it teach?
>
> See, it is gold and silver plated,
>> and there is no breath in it at all.
>
> But the LORD is in his holy temple;
>> let all the earth keep silence before him!
>
> *(Hab. 2:18–20)*

The comparison between the gods worshiped by others and the God of Israel is the difference between gods created by human beings and the God who creates human beings. It is the difference between gods who must be carried around by their worshipers and the God who carries the people. Bel and Nebo were gods worshiped in Babylon. They were statues carved by human beings, carried from place to place on beasts of burden. In contrast, the God of Israel was not created by the people; rather, it was God who called the people and made them a nation. The God of Israel was not carried from place to place by animals, but had carried the people from place to place—from Egypt to the Promised Land, into exile in Babylon—and now was about to carry them back to the Promised Land. Those who worship idols are vainly trying to give life and breath to that which cannot live.

The understanding of God as the Creator is therefore absolutely central. Only such a God can be worshiped as the Lord of all. It is this God who has called a people for the purpose of witnessing to the one true God before the whole world. It is this God, the One who created all things including human beings, who has come among us in the person of Jesus of Nazareth. That is what it means to say that Jesus is Lord.

For many in our culture—and in our church—there is something very arrogant about stating that the God we worship is the only true one and all others are idols. We have some sense that we should assume the gods others worship are as true for them as the God we worship is true for us. To say anything that implies our God is real whereas theirs is not is prejudiced and narrow-minded and leads to persecution.

It is true that the Christian church has waged war on those who worshiped other gods. The Crusades and the conquest of the New World provide more examples of such behavior than we wish to consider. Surely we do not wish to repeat such chapters of our history. Is such persecution a necessary result of our belief in the objective reality of the one true God? No. Such behavior accompanied the combination of church and state, particularly in the later Middle Ages. All churches need to look at clearly and then repent of such behavior in their history and any continuation of such attitudes. It is a sinful misuse of faith, not an obedience to faith. Political power is not a helpful adjunct to the church's proclamation.

At the same time, if Christians assume that the God we worship is not the only God, or that the God we worship did not create all people, then we have compromised the faith we proclaim at its very heart. We also would have no reason to proclaim anything.

When early Christians proclaimed that Jesus is Lord they were speaking a truth they believed was objective, one they themselves subjectively confessed. They proclaimed good news to others and did so without arrogance. The proclamation of the gospel can readily become bad news when it is proclaimed with arrogance rather than love. It is that arrogance combined with political power that leads to persecution.

When the church today proclaims that Jesus is Lord, it is making that claim for all human beings, Christian and non-Christian alike. The fact that Jesus is Lord is the basic content of the gospel we proclaim. We need to learn again how to proclaim the lordship of Christ without arrogance. When the passage from Isaiah quoted above was written, Israel was a captive in Babylon, and Israel was powerless. That was rather like the situation of the early church. In the past several centuries, the Christian church has been dominant in powerful nations and has often used its power to put down other religions. As we move into a more secular society, where the church has less and less connection to power, we have the opportunity to learn again how to proclaim really good news with openness and love.

## The Christian Confession

Early Christians used the term *confession* for the proclamation of their faith. We think of confession as referring to sin. We confess that which is negative about us. We do still use the term "confession of faith" for particular statements that the church has developed, such as the Westminster Confession. In the early church, the individual who was to be baptized made a confession of faith immediately before being baptized. Also, the faithful Christian confessed his or her belief in the face of state persecution and demands for denying Christ. In fact, if such faithful persons survived the persecution, they were called "confessors." (If they did not survive, they were called martyrs.)

This use of the word *confession* both for sin and for faith really shows its full meaning. We confess that which could not be known about us unless we revealed it. A confession is words that reveal. If that which is hidden is a crime or evil, then our words are a confession of sin. If that which is hidden is our commitment to Jesus Christ, then our words are a confession of faith.

Whether of sin or of faith, confession does require words. This points to the fact that a human being is a complex creature who has an inner life, a subjectivity that others cannot know. There is a hidden core in each of us that others can only know if we tell them. We may hide this inner reality from others, and even from ourselves. But for others to know us really, or for us to know ourselves, requires a disclosure, a telling forth, a speaking. The act of revelation from one human being to another is what true intimacy is based on. The act of revelation from God to us is the basis for our intimacy with God. We reciprocate this when we reveal to God, when we confess who God really is and who we really are. God already knows us. God knows us in a way that no human friend can know us. In the process of revealing ourselves to God or to another human being we come to know ourselves. There must be words, even silently spoken in prayer, for this revelation to occur. Our ability to reveal to others who we really are is part of the way in which we are created in the image of God, the One who desires to reveal to us God's own self.

As Christians, we revere the Bible, the written word of God because through it the true God is revealed and therefore seeks intimacy with us. Jesus is called "the Word of God incarnate." He is the supreme revelation of God.

If confession, revelation, of our faith in God to others is the heart of our proclamation, then proclamation is in itself an invitation for others to enter into intimacy not only with God but also with us. There is no way we can proclaim the gospel and invite others to a relationship with God without also being prepared to welcome them into a relationship with us and our congregation. In this way, proclamation is evangelism. Proclamation is part of what is meant by saying that we as the church are the body of Christ in the world. We are the major vehicle by which God through Christ is revealed to others.

In the last chapter we discussed the fact that many church members prefer to let their actions in the community speak about their faith, and hesitate to use words. Confession, however, implies that words are necessary. Actions are never fully self-explanatory. Other people can see our actions but misconstrue our motives. What is true of individuals is true of congregations as well. Confessions are words. Others can imagine the content of our inner life as a church, but only when we speak can they really know who we are. The church proclaims the gospel when it speaks its confession of faith. As the letter of James makes clear, words and actions need to go together (James 2:14–17). Our actions can belie our words, but that does not mean that our words are not needed. In fact, it is dangerous to speak, partly because others can then judge whether our words and our actions correspond.

Confession can be risky. That is clear even in a secular context. If you reveal all your fears and dreams to another human being, you may be rejected, and an intimate relationship may be lost. A person who confesses to a crime runs the risk of legal prosecution. In the realm of faith, there is risk as well. The Theological Declaration of Barmen, included in our *Book of Confessions*, was written by those who were part of what was called the Confessing Church in Germany during the time of Hitler. In response to the Nazi government's request that state churches follow the party line, these Christians declared that Jesus Christ was their only lord, and that they must follow him and not the government. Jesus, not the state, was lord. This was a very dangerous confession of faith to make, and many paid dearly for it. This group was called the Confessing Church because in the face of persecution they confessed their faith that Jesus is Lord.

## Confession as Witness

The cost of faithful confession is seen in the word *martyr*. In the Greek of the New Testament period, martyr simply meant a witness, one called upon to testify in a legal context. It did not mean giving up one's life. But because Christians witnessed to their faith and confessed their faith in the midst of persecution, the word became synonymous with losing one's life for one's beliefs. What these early Christians witnessed to was God's action in Christ, which was the basis for saying that Jesus is Lord. They were not simply asserting that Jesus was the one lord, of many possible lords, that they had decided to claim for themselves. Rather, they confessed their conviction that Jesus was indeed the Lord of all.

In the context of the Roman Empire, this confession of faith meant that the Roman emperor was not lord, nor were the gods worshiped by the empire lords, nor was the empire itself lord. The Christian confession was a political as well as a religious statement, just as the Theological Declaration of Barmen was in Germany in 1934.

In modern English, the word martyr has lost its specifically Christian content and is used both positively and negatively. Positively it refers to those who believe in a cause so much that they willingly lay down their lives for it. Negatively, it refers to an unhealthy psychological condition, the "martyr complex" of people who feel they are always suffering from the callous actions of others. Such people even seek situations where such suffering will occur. For the early church, however, martyrs were chosen by God, and no one could seek such a role or volunteer for it. It was expected that one would take prudent action to avoid persecution, but if it came, one should confess that Jesus is Lord. It was God who called one to such a role. In fact, the phrase in the Lord's Prayer, "lead us not into temptation," can be better translated, "lead us not into a time of trial." Christians knew that their own strength was not sufficient for the test that persecution could bring. They therefore did not choose such trials. Only God could lead them there, with the promise of being with them and giving them the strength they needed. Martyrs were the ultimate witnesses to the power of the gospel. Martyrdoms were proclamation in both word and deed.

The church discovered that though the empire sought to weaken the church through persecution, the church was actually strengthened. Observers of the martyrdoms often were astonished at the faith of those witnesses and sought out the church to discover the source of such triumphant lives. The late-second- to early-third-century North African theologian Tertullian wrote to the Roman authorities in the midst of persecution: "The oftener we are mown down by you, the more in number we grow; *the blood of Christians is seed*."[1]

## Witness to an Easter Faith

Why were martyrdoms such an effective witness? It was not simply that Christians believed so deeply in their cause and this devotion was astonishing to others. Tertullian himself points out that Romans admired devotion to a cause and honored it with statues of their own heroes. Such devotion, though rare among humans, is present outside of the gospel. In the case of Christians, the character of their death was intimately associated with the heart of the gospel itself, which was the astonishing news of the death and resurrection of Jesus Christ.

Proclamation of the Gospel

It was not only that these Christians believed there was indeed life after death. They believed that they were already living the beginning of that life here and now. They had died to their old life and were now living the beginning of their new life in Christ. Furthermore, just as their entire lives of discipleship were a joining in this new, risen life of Christ, their own deaths were a joining in his death as well.

For those catechumens—the ones preparing to be baptized— martyrdom was counted as "baptism in blood." Though they were not yet baptized with water, they were considered to have been baptized when they were martyred. In fact, their baptism was understood to be the real model of baptism—the dying to the old life and rising to the new, dying with Christ and rising with him. In other words, the martyr, at the moment of death, had completed the process of dying to the old life and rising to the new. Those who were baptized with water were beginning the process of dying to the old and rising to the new, but that process would go on throughout their life, until their physical death. They expected that the old life would become weaker and the new life stronger throughout their lifetime. But the martyred catechumen completed both the dying and the rising in the one moment of death.

In the death of Jesus, the old life of the world had been condemned because of its sin. Death was its future. In the resurrection, new life was made possible for those who were incorporated into Christ, those who received the Holy Spirit, those who believed.

What astonished those who saw these Christians die was not how committed they were to their faith, but how victorious they seemed, how even joyful. It was not the joy of those who hated life and wished to leave it, but the joy of those who had found the secret of life. The closest examples we can use in our own day are the reports of those who have had near-death experiences. For many, the clarity that there is life after death means that they no longer fear death as they once did. Their priorities change. They are not as self-protective, as security conscious. Rather, they seek to give to others, to give the greatest priority to loving and caring relationships.

In many respects, the witness of these early Christians was that they too had had a near-death experience. By faith they had died with Christ. They were now living on the other side of death, and could therefore live by new values, no longer seeking their own security. Their ultimate security had been gained for them by Christ. The sign of this new life was above all their ability to love others, even their enemies. Belief in the death and resurrection of Jesus was the heart of their faith. Belief is almost too weak a word, for it was not an intellectual assent to doctrine.

There was an awareness of this new life already growing in the midst of their old life that assured them of the reality of the resurrection. This was the gift, the presence of the Holy Spirit. The resurrection brought them the good news that Jesus has conquered sin and death. Jesus is Lord.

We may have a hard time realizing the full import of Easter for these early disciples. Easter was not the news that there was life after death. Many people already believed that. Many Greeks believed that the soul lives on after death, not because of the resurrection, but because the soul is by its nature immortal. Within the context of Judaism, the Pharisees did believe in the resurrection of the dead at the end of the age, whereas the Sadducees denied it. (See Acts 23:6–10, where Paul uses this difference in his own defense before the Jewish council in Jerusalem.) For both of these groups—the Pharisees and the Greeks —the word of the gospel that there was life after death would not have been news.

The Pharisees and the Christians both believed that there will be a resurrection of the dead, not because we already possess something immortal that cannot die, but by the action of the God who created us in the first place. There was a great difference, however, between what the Pharisees believed and what the Christians proclaimed. The Pharisees still looked for the Messiah who would bring in the end of the age with the resurrection of the dead. The Christians believed that the Messiah had indeed come: Jesus of Nazareth. With him, the end of the age had also come. The new age, the kingdom of God, had entered into our history. Whereas the Pharisees expected the old age to pass away when the new age dawned, the Christians believed that the new age had indeed come, and the resurrection of Jesus was its first witness. What was surprising, even to the earliest Christians, was that while the new age had dawned, the old continued. Those who believed that Christ had indeed risen, believed also that the new age had actually begun. The future was assured.

The gift of the Holy Spirit was further evidence of the kingdom's presence. Those who received the Spirit were enabled to live now on the basis of the life that is the way of the new age. This includes love, humility, joy, and peace. All these virtues are at odds with the character of life in this age, where we seek to preserve our security and avoid anything that would risk it. The Christians who were publicly martyred, confessing their faith in Christ, showed in their deaths these characteristics of the new age. The fact that death did not frighten them, and that even in the midst of death they showed love for one another and even for their enemies, confounded those who persecuted them.

Many who saw them die sought out other Christians so that they could learn the secret of life that these martyrs possessed. What they learned was that the resurrection of Jesus had brought in a new age, which they could now enter. Faith in Christ meant dying to the old life and rising to the new. Baptism was the sign of this transformation. Entering into the water was the sign of dying to the old life. Coming out of the water was the sign of rising to the new life and therefore to the new age as well. Baptism was of enormous significance. It was celebrated with great drama, usually on Easter Eve, the night before Easter Sunday. All the candidates deemed ready for baptism that year were usually baptized on that night, joining in the death and resurrection of Jesus.

The Eucharist also is the feast of this new age that had dawned. In the early church, the Lord's Supper was celebrated every Sunday because that was the Lord's Day—the day of the Lord's resurrection. It was a joyful feast, a celebration of the presence of the risen Lord at Table with his disciples. The account of the disciples on the road to Emmaus (Luke 24:13–35) was the paradigm or the pattern for these celebrations, not the upper room and the shadow of the cross.

Those who received baptism and celebrated the Supper believed that they had been forgiven and enabled to lead a new, transformed life. The Holy Spirit was a reality that transformed their lives. This transformation included the forgiving of others, even enemies. Both baptism and the Lord's Supper were closely related to Good Friday and Easter, with the astonishing news of the resurrection.

## The Rule of Faith

Though the earliest Christians could say what they meant in the simple phrase, "Jesus is Lord," their words implied much more. Since Christianity arose within Judaism, the earliest believers carried with them enormous assumptions that were part of the gospel message. They were clearly monotheistic. They firmly believed that the God who came to us in Jesus of Nazareth was the only God, and that this God had created everything that existed. The creator God was good, and material reality—the earth, our bodies, and animals—also was good. Granted, sin had entered the world and warped this good creation, but that did not change the fact that material reality was good. The same God that created the world also works to free the world from the effects of sin. As part of this work of redemption, God creates a people who can proclaim to the world the will and the plans of God. These early Christians also held to the same understanding of resurrection as Judaism held. Resurrection was a new act of the God who had created us in the first place.

Once the church moved from a largely Jewish population to the Greek and Roman world of the first and second centuries, these assumptions based on Judaism could no longer be guaranteed. Gentile Christians often brought with them their own assumptions, based on the prevailing philosophies of their culture. Among these non-Jewish assumptions that began to come into the church with some new believers was the belief that material things were intrinsically evil and opposed to spiritual reality which was good. Bodies were evil; souls were good. It was on the basis of this belief that the Greek concept of the natural immortality of the soul had been put forward. The God of Jesus Christ therefore could not have been the creator of matter. There was a good redeemer god and an evil creator god. Jesus himself could not have had a body, for he was pure spirit. Therefore, he only appeared to have a body, so human beings could interact with him and hear him. His body was not real. Therefore, he did not need to eat or sleep, he could not have died, and the resurrection was not a real resurrection from the dead.

Because of all of these strange ideas, the church felt it necessary to spell out what the statement "Jesus is Lord" implied. There was no formal meeting, no council or official gathering that wrote out an agreed-upon set of beliefs. In that sense, it was a quite different process than our formal decisions about what should be in our *Book of Confessions.* Rather, the church in each city had what was called "the rule of faith" that listed the various items to be believed, based on the tradition they had received when the gospel was first proclaimed to them. There is great similarity among these statements, partly because there was great interaction among churches. Bishops and other writers of the second century often quote the rule of faith as the basis for their arguments against various heresies. The statements are brief. Candidates for baptism agreed to the rule in order to keep the strange, heretical ideas from coming into the church, and to help all Christians know when a teaching was opposed to the tradition. Each bishop, though elected by the Christians in a city, was actually consecrated by other bishops after circulating among them a statement of his faith. By accepting this statement of faith, the other bishops in the area signified that the new bishop agreed with the understanding of the gospel they all knew and proclaimed.

What did these "rules of faith" include? We have already seen that the resurrection of Jesus was a major part of the meaning that Jesus is Lord. The resurrection assumed that Jesus had died. The resurrection of Jesus cannot be separated from the cross. A truly human death requires a truly human body. The rule of faith added statements about the birth as well as the death of Jesus, in order to make very clear that Jesus was one of us as well as the incarnate Word of the Father. The one who is Lord of all is both God and human. He was born, grew up, suffered, died, and rose again.

Those early Christians who knew Jesus to be Lord knew this because they had experienced the dawning of the kingdom through the gift of the Holy Spirit. Therefore the confession of faith stated clearly the belief in the Holy Spirit, who gives us the power to live this new life. This new life is centered in the church, which is not only the body of Christ but also the community of the Holy Spirit.

When some within the church denied that creation and material reality were good, other statements had to be added to the rule of faith. These had to do with the fact that the same God who came to us in Jesus is also the creator of the world. The same God is both our Creator and our Redeemer.

This outline of the rule of faith may sound familiar to us, and it should. What we know as the Apostles' Creed is basically the rule of faith of the church in the city of Rome, and it dates from the early part of the second century, precisely the time that there was danger from Greek cultural assumptions replacing the Jewish ones upon which the gospel rested.

To be the church, then, is to proclaim to the world that Jesus is Lord, and that the world we live in and we ourselves are the creation of a good God. It also implies that something has happened to this creation and to us so that we are no longer simply that good creation. The whole creation has fallen under the power of sin. Jesus is the way in which God rescues us from the power of sin. His death and resurrection are the central events of this activity. In the cross, Jesus takes on the burden of sin for all of us. On that first Good Friday it appeared to the followers of Jesus that, once again, sin and evil had conquered. But the news of Easter is that Jesus not only took on the burden of our sin but also broke the power of sin and death. His resurrection is the beginning of this new life, lived out from under the power of sin in the world. The Holy Spirit is the power of this new life. The church is the community of this new life.

We will deal with the significance of the gospel in human lives in the next chapter when we discuss the meaning of salvation. But what needs to be clear is that we cannot separate the effects of the gospel from its cause. That is to say, we cannot proclaim the possibility of redemption, of new life, without proclaiming the death and resurrection of Jesus, with all that it implies.

The church has stated its faith, its understanding of the gospel, in the form of confessional statements such as the Apostles' Creed. These statements are used in the midst of our worship services. For many Christians, it is not exactly clear what to do about these statements. When we stand and repeat the Apostles' Creed, or a portion of the Brief Statement of Faith, or other portions of the *Book of Confessions*, are we stating our personal faith or the tradition of the church? What do we do if we do not necessarily completely agree with the statement? Are we hypocrites if we say it? For instance, if the virgin birth, or the ascension, or the second coming is not a clear part of our personal faith, should we keep silent when that part of the Creed is said?

There are several responses to such a question. First, it is above all the faith of the church that we are stating. There is a gospel that is not of our own creating. It has come to us through the church, and not through our own discovery. Second, we need to beware of tailoring the gospel to fit the accepted understandings of the scientific culture in which we live. As we have seen, believing only that which is already agreed to by our society means the gospel has really nothing new to say. It is not news at all. Fourth, we need to be aware of the reasons why the church has understood its faith in this way. We need to ask: What is at stake? Why does it matter?

When we have looked at these issues, it may be possible to say that certain things are part of the church's proclamation, but that we do not fully understand them. We are then committed to further study and discussion on these issues. Most of us reject various doctrines before we study them and know what is really meant. Nor do we readily communicate our doubts to others in the congregation. If we did, we might find issues that really are of concern to many, and that therefore should be studied by the congregation. All these questions relate to the basic issue of the authority of the individual and the authority of the church.

### The Means of Proclamation: Invitation

To proclaim is to reveal our own faith in Jesus as Lord. To reveal our inmost life, our life of faith, is to invite others into a relationship of intimacy with us. The gospel we are proclaiming speaks of new life that has begun even now for those who believe, who understand what God has done in Christ. If this is the content of the gospel we proclaim, what does it say about how we proclaim it? Are there means of communication that deny the content? Are there means that support the content?

To proclaim the gospel is to invite others to enter into the community of faith. These elements cannot be separated. A community of faith is a congregation, an actual gathering of God's people. To proclaim the gospel in a way that does not include an invitation to join us—a real live congregation—is somehow not congruent, not appropriate for the gospel. It makes it appear that the Christian faith is simple a matter of believing certain things. One can do that in response to an ad, a pamphlet, a radio broadcast. Perhaps such communications urge their readers or hearers to find a church to attend. But it still is a distant invitation, rather like inviting someone to find a friend to have dinner with. That is not really an invitation. Jesus is the one who invites, ultimately, but the invitation is issued through us, the body of Christ, and it is an invitation to become part of us. The most effective proclamation is the direct invitation by a congregation that is clearly willing and open to such new membership.

Congregations are not always ready to issue such invitations. They are therefore not really ready for evangelistic proclamation. There are a variety of reasons why congregations may not be ready to issue an invitation to faith in Christ, an invitation that involves joining their congregation. New people would share in decision-making, and perhaps those who have been accustomed to leadership are not ready for that, especially if the decisions might be different than they would have made. The congregation may be very close-knit, and may find it difficult to add many new members without weakening the sense of community.

These are understandable reasons. But if the unity of the congregation is based on the new life which the resurrection provides, if the gospel is the reason for the existence of the congregation and for the new members joining, then that unity would help enormously in integrating old and new members, and the decision-making of the congregation would be on the basis of the common gospel. A congregation is evangelistic if it can clearly articulate the gospel that is the basis of its members' life together, and if it is open to proclaim that gospel so that new people can be added to the congregation on the basis of common faith. A congregation that seeks to be truly evangelistic must be focused above all on the gospel it has to proclaim to the world, knowing that such proclamation involves a sincere invitation to all who believe to join as full members of the congregation. It also involves inviting those who are interested to come and try out such a life in order to decide.

## Virtual Congregations?

In our own day we have many possibilities for communication that the church in previous generations could not even imagine. Two in particular need to be mentioned: television and the Internet. We can watch a church service on television, a full congregation at worship. Even if we faithfully watched every Sunday, would we really be part of that congregation? What would we be missing? We are hearing the message, and we are able to respond personally—that is, individually. If we were to join in an internet "chat room" that sought to be a congregation, would it really be one? If the people never met face to face, if their only interaction was what they chose to reveal at a distance, would that really be a Christian community?

In one sense, the church is like a family. We grow up in families, and then often scatter because of schools, jobs, and marriages. We are at a distance from those we love. We use forms of communication such as the Internet, or the telephone, videos, or letters. All of these are great helps at preserving the ties. But they are preserving ties that once were face to face, and that may be again in the future. We know each other from our previous life together, and now we are maintaining those ties through these other means. It is a totally different question to have an entire relationship without ever meeting. We know then only a small part of the life of the other. We have no way to know how their words and their lives go together. We lack the wider knowledge of the person that would let us truly interpret their words. It is only a part of the person and not the whole person to whom we are relating by such means. We may prefer it because it is less demanding, or because we know that what we say or write will never get back to the people who really know us. In that sense, the intimacy of common confession is not really present. The concept of "virtual congregations" needs to be questioned very severely.

It is a different situation for the person who has been an active part of a congregation and now is prevented from being present physically because of illness or a similar situation. Then the congregation, like a family, needs to find ways of including the person. Persons can be included through visitation by members of the congregation, by receiving Communion as a part of the congregation, by being part of prayer groups or prayer chains when possible, and by using the telephone, the Internet, tape recorders, or whatever else keeps them from being isolated.

Even though we have stressed the significance of the congregation, there needs to be a further caveat. The person who is homebound because of illness is not the same as the person who has moved away, who would be perfectly able to become part of another congregation, but prefers to continue membership in the previous one, at a distance. Christians need the church. They need living congregations they interact with frequently, on a weekly or even daily basis. In a new community they need to find a new congregation because they can no longer gather with the previous one. Of course friendships remain, and there are ties that continue. But Christians without congregations in which they are active members are like fish without water: they will not survive for long. They will turn the Christian faith into an individualized set of beliefs rather than the living experience of being part of the new creation.

The church is both extremely local, gathered into congregations that meet face to face, and at the same time it is global. We use the word "church" in the singular both for the local congregation and for the worldwide reality of the Christian community. One of the major reasons the church was persecuted in the early centuries was precisely because it was seen as an empire-wide institution, and really the only challenge to the empire itself as a source of unity among diverse peoples. Though it was an extreme minority, it quickly spread around the Mediterranean basin. Bishops kept in touch with one another in local gatherings, and maintained contact with others more distant through letters. We have seen the significance of this in the development of the rule of faith. To be truly Christian, one had to be connected with Christians in all the other places. Because the Roman Empire had secured the safety of the roads and the Mediterranean Sea, commerce was extensive. Christians traveled to other cities and felt it absolutely necessary to find a congregation there with whom they could gather while they were in town. There were common meals that included these visitors. All congregations seemed like extensions of their home congregation.

The church as the body of Christ cannot be divided into independent units that have no connection with each other. There is a drive for unity in the nature of the Christian faith. The ecumenical movement is based on this reality, seeking to overcome the modern phenomenon of denominationalism. We cannot assume that Christians of other denom-inations are not part of the body of Christ. It is interesting that the rule of faith always includes a statement about "the one holy catholic church." It is an act of faith to believe that these various gatherings of Christians throughout the world, different as they are, are "the church." People who move permanently from one town to another and can no longer worship with their previous congregation should feel a need to become actively involved with a new one. The local and the world-wide are both characteristics of the Christian church.

## The Barriers

There are several barriers in our own day to our proclamation of the gospel as invitation to become part of a community of the resurrection, of the new creation.

### Individualism

The first barrier is a problem we have already mentioned: individualism. Our culture is so permeated with individualism that we find the thought of our need for the church to be highly suspect. Nor are we convinced others need us in order to be Christians. For many, Christianity is a matter of what we do individually, what we believe, how we act. The church may need us, and a congregation may need new members in order to survive as a social institution, but as Christians, do we really need the church? The church may have many mission projects and programs and need members in order to carry them out, but do the members have the sense that they need the church? A hymn that was popular in the past, and that has been largely unused recently because of its gender-specific language, is "Rise Up, O Men of God." But more problematic than the language itself is the idea the hymn expresses that the church is weak and waiting for us to come to its aid. This reverses the situation as the early church understood it. It is we who stand in need of the church, not the other way around.

Closely related to individualism is the perception that Christianity is really nothing more than a set of ethical standards. Those who live according to these standards are really Christians, whether or not they profess any faith in Jesus Christ. We see this misunderstanding in action when people assume that to say someone is not a Christian is really some sort of insult, reflecting badly on his or her morality—even if the person in question is a devout Hindu or Muslim. Christians do not have a monopoly on good moral standards. Obviously, to be a Christian does involve living ethically. But that is not the uniqueness of Christianity.

### The Loss of Newness

A second barrier is the loss of the sense of the real newness of faith, the real presence of the new age in our midst. Much of the early Christians' understanding of the gospel assumed this experience of the dawning of the kingdom of God in their midst. That was very true for

Christians when they were a small and powerless group within the vast Roman Empire. However, beginning in the fourth century, when the church abruptly became the dominant and almost exclusive religious institution of the Roman Empire, that began to change. In fact, considering that the greatest persecution occurred just before the church was adopted by the empire, it is no wonder that many Christians saw the empire's friendship as a sign of the kingdom.

The most comprehensive persecution of Christians began in A.D. 303. The church was at that time very much a minority but well known. The persecution ended when the new emperor, Constantine, issued the Edict of Toleration in 313. That edict permitted all religions freedom to worship. But Constantine had great hopes that the unity of the church would bring about a renewed sense of the unity of the empire itself, and that other religions would gradually die out. Therefore, though all religions were permitted, Constantine favored the church, giving it access to the imperial postal service, tax exemption, and draft exemption for Christian clergy. These privileges were not extended to other religious groups. Constantine also declared Sunday to be a holiday, and he began building churches. To many Christians, the change from the fearsome time of persecution was so astonishing, they began to think that the Roman Empire was the present form of the kingdom, and that whatever remained to be experienced would have to wait until after death. The loss of a real experience of newness had arrived with Constantine.

Because of the empire's support, many people wished to join the church, many more than the church could really handle with its earlier thorough training for baptismal candidates. Many people joined with little real preparation. Therefore, many cultural assumptions drawn from Greek, non-Christian sources began to enter into the church, including the idea of the immortality of the soul as opposed to the Jewish understanding of resurrection of the dead. Where this became dominant, it was hard to see Jesus' resurrection as something other than the verification of life after death. There was little to be said about a new creation.

In the western part of the empire, a new crisis was beginning in the fifth century—invasion and conquest by the Germanic tribes. Through various missionary efforts, these peoples were added to the church. However, they too had cultural assumptions that affected the understanding of the gospel. They were particularly interested in how individuals were freed from the need to pay in suffering for the sins they had committed. The gospel was tailored to answer this question.

By the later Middle Ages, almost everyone was Christian. Baptism was understood as an individual matter, bringing forgiveness of sin. Normally, infants were baptized within two weeks of birth, since all were children of Christian parents. Sins after baptism would be dealt with through confession to the priest and carrying out the penance assigned. Communion was understood to be a reenactment of the death of Christ as a sacrifice for sin. It had more to do with Good Friday than with Easter. The kingdom of God was only to be expected after death and judgment.

The Protestant Reformation rejected much of this understanding, particularly any reenactment of the death of Christ in the Eucharist. Nor did they believe that baptism dealt only with sins up to that point, and confession to a priest was needed thereafter. Granted that these are significant changes, still it is clear that most Protestant groups, including our own Reformed tradition, did little to recover the sense that a new age had broken into our world in the resurrection of Jesus. Most churches were official state churches and had the support of the society. Furthermore, it was assumed that everyone born within that nation would be a member of the state church. The few exceptions were usually severely persecuted.

We can see the change from the Easter faith of the early church in several ways. Many of us who grew up in the Presbyterian Church before the 1960s remember Communion services that were quite funereal in tone. The hymns that we sang at Communion were Good Friday hymns: "In the Cross of Christ I Glory" and "When I Survey the Wondrous Cross." Baptisms were almost always of infants, and they were individualistic in character, or else a family affair, scheduled when grandparents and other relatives could be present. New members could be readily added with little training, since it was assumed that everyone in the society really knew what the church proclaimed. It was only necessary that they make a decision to accept it.

## Signs of Hope

More recently, there has been a significant recovery of the early theology, with its stress on the new creation, the kingdom, which entered our history with the resurrection of Christ. There is a new emphasis on the connection of the Lord's Supper and Easter, and new appreciation for the significance of baptism for the whole life of the church, not just for the individual. A brief look at the hymns suggested for Communion in the new *Presbyterian Hymnal* reveals many references to the resurrection, the living presence of the Lord, and not only a looking back at the cross. The Lord's Supper is celebrated much more frequently now, often once a month instead of once a quarter. Attendance used to go down on Communion Sundays. That is no longer the case.

These are hopeful signs, but often these changes come about in a congregation without any clear understanding of the theological changes that lie behind them. Why is there now a renewal of this early theology? With the great increase in secularism that is typical of most Western societies, and with the enormous religious diversity because of immigration, we who were the inheritors of Constantine's support of the church are finding ourselves much more in the situation of those early Christians, before the time of Constantine. That does not mean we are being persecuted. More often, we are being ignored as irrelevant.

For whatever reason, there is decreasing social pressure for people to join the church. Those who have little or no commitment to the faith can quite easily drop out of church life or never be a part of it at all. With secularization, there is a new audience for the church's proclamation: those who have grown up outside the church and really have never heard the gospel. This is a radically new situation for most mainline churches. It used to be that even parents who had no real interest in the church at least had their children baptized. Congregations that have recovered a sense of the significance of baptism are no longer willing to baptize such children. In future years there will be more and more unbaptized people in our society, the children of both secular parents and of immigrants from traditionally non-Christian societies. Already many Presbyterian congregations are baptizing more adults. A generation ago many Presbyterians never saw an adult being baptized because almost all children had been baptized. These adult converts often enter the church because they have heard something new, something life-transforming. They have much to teach many of us, who have been in the church all of our lives, about the surprising good news of the gospel.

We call this transformation "salvation." The first Great End of the Church calls for the proclamation of the gospel for the purpose of salvation. What is this salvation the gospel proclaims? In the next chapter we will examine that question.

---

Note

1. Tertullian, "Apology" and "The Five Books Against Marcion" in the *Ante-Nicene Fathers*, vol. iii, Master Christian Library (8th ed. CD-ROM), Kansas City, MO: L & C Software, Ages Digital Library, 2000.

# Study Questions

1. What does González mean when she says that when the church becomes part of a culture, often the message it offers becomes all too believable? Why is this a problem?

2. González notes that it is essential to understand that God is the Creator of the whole world and that it is this same God who has come to live among us in the person of Jesus of Nazareth. Yet to some Christians it feels wrong to proclaim that Jesus Christ is Lord of all. Describe this tension. Do you feel it yourself?

3. The power that the gospel proclaims as good news is not arrogant or domineering. How does this impact the way we might proclaim the gospel? How might our proclamation of the gospel be arrogant?

4. How is the gospel related to self-knowledge? How is a relationship with others a part of the proclamation of the gospel?

5. How is the gospel "good news" if it means dying? Describe the joy of the ancient martyrs. In what ways do you understand following Christ as witness today? What does it mean for you to die with Christ? How is it new life? In what ways is witness different now than it was in its early days? What is the freedom gained? What is lost?

6. What assumptions do we as North American congregations bring to our hearing of the gospel?

7. What do you think about the rule of faith? What comparable tools do we have in the Presbyterian Church (U.S.A.)?

8. Why does González say that it is we who stand in need of the church and not the other way around, if the church is indeed losing members?

9. How is the gospel the basis for unity? Have you experienced this unity, perhaps as your congregation deals with difference of views among its members?

10. Why is it important for Christians to be active members of congregations in all senses possible? Do you feel a tension in your own life between your private or personal commitments and the commitments of your congregation? How do you resolve them?

11. Persecution of the Christian church ceased when Constantine issued the Edict of Toleration in A.D. 313. People were relieved from previous dangers related to their faith. Describe the reaction

of the people and talk about how this same situation of freedom of religion here in the United States compares with that of Constantine's time.

12. How might a renewal of the sense of a new creation or of the kingdom of God happen in your church today? What are the barriers to this renewal? What are some signs of hope?

# "For the Salvation . . ."

# 3

The first Great End of the Church makes it clear that the gospel is proclaimed so that salvation happens. What, then, do we mean by salvation? For many Presbyterians, the word *salvation* is tied to a very particular understanding. Conservative evangelists ask the question, "Are you saved?" and expect a simple yes or no answer. The theology behind such a question is that salvation has to do with going to heaven after death, and thereby avoiding hell. The way of salvation is to accept Jesus as the one who saves us because of his sacrificial death that paid the penalty for our sins. For some Presbyterians this is a familiar and accurate way to describe the gospel and the meaning of salvation.

Other Presbyterians are uncomfortable with this response. Therefore, they also avoid any discussion of salvation since there seems to be no other meaning for the word salvation than the one just described. Yet it is hard to imagine the proclamation of the gospel without a sense that the gift of salvation is at the heart of the effort. The death of Jesus on the cross is intimately connected with salvation. The question is whether this is the only element of the work of Christ that is related to our salvation.

The New Testament and the early church had a far broader way of expressing the significance of the work of Christ in human life. We lose a great deal when we narrow the focus to the state of our life after death. In the same way that there have been recent changes—and expansions—of our understanding of baptism and the Lord's Supper, as we saw in the last chapter, so also there has been a recapturing of the wider meaning of salvation. We need to explore these various meanings more thoroughly, not to choose one among them and reject the rest, but to understand the fullness of the work of Christ that cannot be limited to a single expression.

The narrowing of the church's understanding of the meaning of salvation results in narrowing our biblical view as well. If we look again at the list of the Great Ends of the Church, we need to remember that they are all interconnected. What salvation means includes the creation of the community of faith, in which we are sheltered and nurtured as the children of God. Salvation creates our spiritual fellowship and leads us to worship the one true God. It is the truth about salvation we are called upon to maintain. Salvation gives us the vision of what social righteousness looks like, and it empowers us to live by such a vision. Salvation gives us new eyes to see God's intentions for creation, the goal God has, that is the kingdom of heaven, so that even now, in halting ways, we can exhibit it to the world. Therefore, the meaning of salvation has to be understood in ways that lead to all the Great Ends.

## The Scope of Salvation

The theology behind the simple question, "Are you saved?" is quite different from much of the early church's theology. For one thing, it is highly individualistic. The question asks about my salvation, my decision, and leaves out several crucial issues. Neither the resurrection of Jesus nor the role of the church seems to be significant as part of the means of salvation. Nor is there a sense that salvation concerns an inbreaking of the new creation in the midst of our present life and not only a word about life after death. Furthermore, the question often is cast in a way that is more bad news than good. The basic message seems to be that we must believe the evangelist's message or go to hell.

However, there is obviously some truth in the question such an evangelist asks. Our salvation is related to the death of Christ. Salvation does promise a glorious future to those who are in Christ. All of this is good news. But the modern individualism, the loss of the sense of the new creation now, these are deficiencies that must be overcome. Even in theology that centers on the death of Christ as payment for sin, there is often an emphasis on the work of the Holy Spirit, made possible by the death and resurrection of Christ. The Holy Spirit brings new life. However, this is often viewed in an individualistic fashion. We shall come back to the work of the Spirit in the Christian life.

What then is the meaning of salvation, a meaning that really brings good news to the world? The word for salvation in Greek means health and wholeness. It includes the healing or health of more than the individual: the health of a society, and the wholeness of our lives as families and communities are also implied. The word salvation is used not only for entrance into eternal life but also deliverance from enemies, from sickness, from oppressive conditions. In our own language we speak of saving a life or being saved from disaster. Salvation involves the wholeness of life as God intends it.

Christians often use the term "redemption" in generally the same way as salvation. The word "liberation" also has some currency. In the Psalms we find the term "deliverance" used constantly. In each case of each word, the term has a cognate used to describe Jesus: Savior, Redeemer, Liberator, Deliverer. These terms agree that Jesus has saved, redeemed, liberated, or delivered us from something. That something can be defined in different ways. Are we freed from paying the penalty for our sins and therefore from condemnation after death? Are we freed from the power of evil, here and now, as well as later? Are we freed from slavery to sin and death? Are we freed from an old life to a new, abundant life? Are we freed from an old creation to be participants in a new creation?

There are many passages in Scripture, very significant for understanding the work of Christ in our lives, that are often overlooked when we seek to comprehend the meaning of salvation. In light of the perceived conflict between science and the Bible, some passages are debated only on the question "could they have happened?" or "did they happen exactly as stated?" The question of what the biblical author is telling us about the work of salvation is overlooked or lost in the midst of a debate that was not in the mind of the authors. Part of the task we face is looking more comprehensively at Scripture when we form our view of salvation. Let us look now at several passages we do not always consider in regard to the meaning of salvation.

## From What Are We Saved?

Salvation needs to be defined partly in terms of that from which we are being saved. Stemming from the Jewish background of the church, early Christians had a firm belief that though this world was the creation of God and therefore good, it was also under the power of sin. Something had happened. The story of the Garden of Eden in Genesis 3 is descriptive of this belief. Creation is good, but the world we live in is not exactly the same world that God created.

Nor is it only human beings that have suffered. Within the brief verses of Genesis 3 we find that the earth has changed, symbolized by the growth of thorns and thistles, making life difficult. Pain in childbirth is another way of saying that the human body is not exactly the way God created it either. Not that we were intended to live forever in this world, but pain and disease that are the result of physical malfunctioning of the body are the present human condition and not the way God intended things to be. Later in Genesis (Gen. 9:1–7), when Noah and his family are told that they may eat meat, in contrast to Gen. 1:29–30, where both animals and humans ate only plants, we are told that the fear between wild animals and human beings is also not the way God wished it. We eat animals and they eat each other. There is a violence in the whole of creation now that Genesis tells us was not part of God's good creation. It is, however, the way things are. It is also interesting that the covenant that is described between Noah and God includes not only Noah's descendants; the covenant includes all the species of animals that Noah had rescued in the ark (Gen. 9:10). That is a detail we often overlook. God's concern is for more than the salvation of human beings. It is a concern for the whole creation. We see the same concern in the story of Jonah, the unwilling prophet, who is sent to the enemy city of Nineveh to proclaim the need for repentance. When Jonah is angry because God has saved the city, God's response is that God's concern was not only for the Ninevites, but also for the many animals in the city (Jon. 3:11).

For more than a millennium, Christians have generally been tempted to narrow the focus of God's work of salvation not only to human beings alone, but also only to the spiritual, nonphysical part of the human being, usually called the soul. It was the influence of Greek rather than biblical thought that created such a narrowing. The Bible views the scope of God's concern far more widely. It is the whole of God's creation that needs redemption, not only the human portion. As we saw in the passages from Genesis, the whole creation fell, not only human beings. Violence and death have entered into the scene for animals as well as people. What Charles Darwin in the nineteenth century called "the survival of the fittest" is a description of this violence that causes weaker creatures to become the prey of stronger ones. What Genesis 9 tells us is that this process is not part of the good creation of God but the result of the corruption of that creation because of human sin.

There is no simple cure for this violence. I as an individual may decide I will not participate in it. I may even decide I will become a vegetarian. But I cannot, with all the good will in the world, stop the wolf from eating the sheep. I may use the best gardening techniques around, but I cannot stop the thorns and thistles, or their local equivalents, from invading my garden if I leave it to nature alone. What Genesis is telling us is that the whole creation, human beings, animals, the earth itself, have fallen under a power that has shaped them in ways that are contrary to the good Creator's original intentions. Though Genesis also says that this corruption of the creation is due in some mysterious way to human sin, and that it occurs under the providence of God, it is also clear that individual decisions to lead a moral life are not going to cure the situation. It is beyond human power, individually or collectively.

Israel's understanding of the future kingdom points to the over-coming of this fallennesss in creation itself, as in Isaiah's vision of the "peaceable kingdom" (Isa. 11:6–9; 65:25). Both the Old Testament and the New point to a future hope that includes the creation itself, and not just human beings.

If the power of sin is so extensive that it makes human bodies susceptible to pain and disease, alters the earth itself so that life is difficult, causes violence and fearfulness among animals, then the work of salvation is also far greater than we might have imagined. That is what the church understood in its early days. Paul captures this in his letter to the Christians at Rome, when he speaks of the futility under which the whole creation now is (Rom. 8:18–39). He also makes the astonishing statement that this widespread corruption of the creation was the will of God. That does not mean that God wished it to be this way, but that God evidently wished that the result of human sin would be this great. Sinful human beings, which we all are, must live in a world that is not perfect, a world that reflects our own condition of estrangement from the Creator.

We often forget this fall of creation. Presbyterians generally admit that human beings are sinful, but we assume that whatever is is "natural" and therefore the way God created things to be. What do we mean by natural? We usually mean that which occurs in nature, without our intervention. But if the whole creation was affected by the fall, then what occurs "naturally" needs to be seen as part of the character of a fallen creation and not necessarily as part of God's intention for a good creation.

If the need for salvation is so extensive, what does this say about the work of Jesus as Savior? There are several passages that point to this wide work of redemption, wider than our individual state of being after death. For instance, consider this familiar passage in the gospel: the calming of the storm at sea (Matt. 8:23–27). This shows the power of Jesus over nature itself. He is indeed the Lord of all creation. Two particular instances of healing also need to be considered. In Mark 2:1–12, we are told of a paralytic who was lowered by four friends into the room where Jesus was healing people. Jesus heals him by saying, "Your sins are forgiven." When the crowd protests that only God can forgive sins, Jesus replies: "Which is easier, to say to the paralytic, 'Your sins are forgiven,' or to say, 'Stand up and take your mat and walk'? But so that you may know that the Son of Man has authority on earth to forgive sins"—he said to the paralytic—"I say to you, stand up, take your mat and go to your home" (Mark 2:9–11).

What is clear in this passage is that there is some deep connection between sin and illness. Lest we think that it is a simple connection—we individually sin and are struck with illness—we need also to read the passage in John 9:1–3, where Jesus is asked whether a man was born blind because of his own sin or because of the sin of his parents. Jesus replies: "Neither this man nor his parents sinned; he was born blind so that God's works might be revealed in him." In other words, we cannot make a direct connection between a particular person's ailment and his or her own sin. In Luke 13:1–5, Jesus speaks of the tower of Siloam, which fell and killed eighteen people. He reminded them that those eighteen were no worse sinners than others in Galilee. Disasters and diseases do not occur on the basis of individual sinfulness. They are part of the whole human lot.

What strange passages. The miracles of Jesus point to who he is, the Lord of creation. They point to the work of Christ freeing not only us but the whole creation from bondage to sin. This will not occur completely in this age, which is why we dare not let the lions and the lambs lie down together, no matter how much goodwill we have.

Many of us look at such passages and decide they make no sense in our scientifically ordered world. We know why pain occurs in childbirth, and we are able to take measures to prevent or alleviate it. We know what causes disease, and we are working to cure the various ailments that trouble humanity. We know the causes of so many things, and we are seeking to discover others. The biblical understanding seems totally irrelevant to our lives.

The picture that the Bible presents is beyond the scope of modern science. It is answering other questions than the ones we ask science. We do not have to choose either science or Scripture, and deny the other. Science does tell us the causes of various diseases and physical problems. It does show us the violence that is the "food chain" within which we live. What the biblical picture shows us is why a good Creator allowed such problems to occur in the midst of a good creation, and what God's ultimate intentions are. Science seeks cures for various problems, and that is good. But science cannot break the whole creation free from the power of sin under which it lies. Science can tell us what is natural in our present situation, but it cannot tell us what God's good creation was intended to be. That must come from God, the Creator and Redeemer of this world.

Salvation has wide implications. They include the healing of bodies and minds and the concern for the nonhuman creation. These issues raise many questions that Presbyterians are struggling with in our own day.

## Faith and Healing

Salvation or redemption is related to illness. Presbyterians have been extremely cautious about the connection between faith and healing. We have generally distrusted what has been called "faith healing." There are good reasons for this. Though many human ailments are caused by our own foolish behavior, and faith may well help us overcome the bad habits that lead to ill health, we are generally clear that a great deal of human misery and sickness is not related to our personal actions. Even Christians with great personal faith still live in a fallen world.

Imagine a child who is born with a congenital heart defect. We do not believe that this child or the parents sinned and are being punished by this event. Granted, the parents are sinful, as are all human beings. Even the child has the propensity to sin as part of the human condition. But we do not draw a simple line between their sinfulness and the problem the child faces. Nor do we believe that if the parents had enough faith, their child would be healed.

So much for what we do not believe. What do we proclaim and believe in such situations? We believe that, though this world has fallen under the power of evil, so that the creation is not exactly what God willed, God is with us in the midst of all that happens. Faith does not spare Christians from the common woes of humanity, but it does give us the strength to believe in the power of God's grace to uphold us and our children in all that happens. We do not believe that the faithful can overcome by their faith the problems to which flesh is now heir. That is a part of the message of some "faith-healing" groups that we absolutely oppose.

At the same time, such groups have glimpsed something of the wider meaning of salvation that we often have overlooked. We know we do not believe that illness can be cured by faith rather than by science, but after that, we are not at all clear what our faith should lead us to do or to believe in regard to illness. Yet the salvation gained through Jesus Christ does speak to this area of human life. What should we do? Should we accept whatever occurs, bow to the will of God, and ask for strength? Can we pray that God will cure the person who is ill, even though it seems unlikely in medical terms that such a healing could occur? Of course we can, and ask others to pray as well—always, however, with the understanding that a cure is not a test of the strength of our faith. We can also pray that the medical team will be strengthened and guided, that scientists will find a cure, that the person suffering will be given the grace that whatever happens, their faith will be strengthened and not weakened. We can pray that the relationships of all who are involved will be strengthened and healed in this time of testing.

There is a model for us in Paul's words in 2 Corinthians 12:7b–9a: "To keep me from being too elated, a thorn was given to me in the flesh, a messenger of Satan to torment me, to keep me from being too elated. Three times I appealed to the Lord about this, that it would leave me, but he said to me, 'My grace is sufficient for you, for power is made perfect in weakness.' " Paul prayed for healing, and yet, though he was faithful, it did not happen. Whatever the weakness was, it had no effect on God's grace being active and manifest in Paul's life. In all of our situations, we can proclaim the sense of victory even in the midst of sorrow that Paul proclaims at the end of the eighth chapter of Romans: "I am convinced that neither death, nor life, nor angels, nor rulers, nor things present, nor things to come, nor powers, nor height, nor depth, nor anything else in all creation, will be able to separate us from the love of God in Christ Jesus our Lord" (Rom. 8:38–39).

In recent years, the Presbyterian Church has developed "services of wholeness" that include prayers for healing. These are to be found in the *Book of Common Worship.* In some congregations, such services occur weekly, in others monthly, in others, occasionally. Many congregations are not even aware that these possibilities exist. These services point to the wider understanding of salvation that is being recaptured. It would be helpful for a session or congregation to look seriously at such services, and to discuss the understanding of salvation that lies behind them. A study could be carried out without any assumption that such a service would be held, though that might be a result. The study itself would raise the question of the wider scope of salvation.

Presbyterians have been in the forefront of bringing the message of the gospel along with medical missions to other parts of the world. We have not been as clear in our own home congregations, when articulating the connection between the gospel and human health. Salvation does point to health in body, in mind, in family relationships, in society, in ecology. The church of Jesus Christ has every reason to be concerned with all these areas.

## Faith and Ecology

In recent years, there has been increasing concern about the pollution of the water and the air, the destruction of animal habitats, the depleting of natural resources, the thinning of the ozone layer, and so forth. Sometimes these issues have been cast in terms of justice, particularly the need to consider the effects of these ecological changes on human beings around the world, or on human beings in the generations that come after us. All of this is true, and is an important basis for altering our destructive ways. But there are theological reasons for our concern. We share the planet with others who are also God's creatures, and God is interested in them as well as in us. God's covenant and God's actions for salvation are related to the whole of creation, not only to human beings.

At some level we have always known this. Why do so many Christmas cards include the illustration of the lion and the lamb lying down together? They do so because the birth of the Savior is related to making such a vision a reality. Why are we so fascinated with statues of St. Francis and the birds? We have some sense that God's purposes include harmony in all of creation, between animals that now prey upon one another, as well as between wild animals and human beings.

When Paul wrote to the Corinthians about the transformation that salvation brings to a person, he wrote, "If anyone is in Christ, there is a new creation: everything old has passed away; see, everything has become new!" (2 Cor. 5:17). We often read this as meaning that the one who is redeemed has become a new creation. But that is not what the text is saying. Rather, it says that for the one who is redeemed, the one who is now in Christ, the whole creation has become new; that is, the whole creation is now seen with new eyes.

## The Role of Human Beings

Why should human sin lead to changes in the whole creation? From the point of view of the whole biblical narrative, we need to realize the position within creation that God intended human beings to hold. There are three passages in particular that point to this role. The first passage is in Genesis 1. It has been the source of debate in recent years. Genesis 1:28 reads: "God blessed them [male and female], and God said to them, "Be fruitful and multiply, and fill the earth and subdue it; and have dominion over the fish of the sea and over the birds of the air and over every living thing that moves upon the earth."

Since we have become aware of the ecological crisis, there has been a great deal of discussion as to the significance of this dominion that human beings were given in the original good creation. Some have argued that the whole concept of dominion is a bad one. They see it pointing to the power that human beings have exercised over creation, forgetting that human beings are also creatures. On the basis of this dominion, so the argument goes, human beings have exploited the rest of creation for their own benefit. Some have even viewed this text from Genesis 1 as the source of the ecological crisis itself, and blame biblical religions for much of the current problem.

The second passage, in Psalm 8, makes a clear reference to Genesis 1:28:

> What are human beings that you are mindful of them,
>
> > mortals that you care for them?
>
> Yet you have made them a little lower than God,
>
> > and crowned them with glory and honor.
>
> You have given them dominion over the works of your hands;
>
> > you have put all things under their feet.
>
> *(Ps. 8:4–6)*

The early church understood dominion to mean that human beings were the crown of God's creation, creatures like all the rest, but the highest of the creatures. In fact, the harmony of all the creation depended upon human beings relating properly to the Creator. We have consciousness, voices, ways to praise God on behalf of all the rest of creation. In a sense, human beings were intended to bring the praise of all creation to God, almost as though human beings were the priests before God for the whole nonhuman creation.

Therefore when human beings turned away from their Creator in sin, the effects were profound for all the rest of the creation, precisely because of the place human beings held. If there is no peace and harmony between the crown of creation and the Creator, there will be discord and violence throughout the creation. Human dominion was for peace, not for exploitation. Our exploitation of the rest of creation, which has indeed occurred, is a sign of our sin, not of our proper dominion.

We may find this a strange, archaic understanding. It is not a description of a scientific process but of the purpose and reality of God's intentions for the world. In fact, to put it in terms of science is to lessen and deny the great truths this biblical description is intended to convey. Science describes what is; Genesis 1 and Psalm 8 describe what was intended and still remains God's purpose for the world. The Bible knows very well that what was intended is not the current situation. In what is, it may agree with a scientific view. But unlike human wisdom alone, the Bible declares that it is human sin that has caused the present, violent reality, and that overcoming the powers that keep us from abundant life is in God's hands and not ours. It involves an end to the power of sin under which the whole creation lies.

The third passage is in the New Testament, Hebrews 2:5–9. This is a more complex passage and needs to be looked at carefully. It begins with a word about the future: "Now God did not subject the coming world, about which we are speaking, to angels." The issue is about who shall have dominion in the future world, that is, the kingdom of God. Granted, God has supreme dominion, but the author is asking whether humans or angels are to have dominion in the future. Angels play an important part as agents of God. John Calvin wrote that we are not to imagine angels as literally having wings. He wrote that the description of wings was given in order to assure us that God's help could reach us quickly, as soon as we needed it.[1]

Earlier in this letter the author had written, "Are not all angels spirits in the divine service, sent to serve for the sake of those who are to inherit salvation?" (1:14). In other words, though at the present time human beings are lesser creatures than angels, in the future it is human beings who will have dominion, the dominion they were created to have but forfeited because of sin. This is similar to Paul's understanding that until the redemption gained in Christ, human beings were like children, under the care of tutors. But their destiny was to be far greater than that of the tutors (Gal. 3:23—4:7).

The author continues, evidently quoting Psalm 8 from memory: "But someone has testified somewhere, 'What are human beings that you are mindful of them, or mortals, that you care for them? You have made them for a little while lower than the angels; you have crowned them with glory and honor, subjecting all things under their feet.' " So far this is generally a parallel to the Genesis 1 and Psalm 8 passages, stating the place of human beings in the whole scheme of God's creation. In the future world, we will have dominion. We were created for that. But then the author goes on to consider our present situation, reflecting the reality of our disordered existence:

> Now in subjecting all things to them [human beings], God
> left nothing outside their control. As it is, we do not yet
> see everything in subjection to them, but we do see Jesus,
> who for a little while was made lower than the angels,
> now crowned with glory and honor because of the
> suffering of death, so that by the grace of God he might
> taste death for everyone. *(Heb. 2:8–9)*

All things were to be under human dominion, but it is clear that such is not the case at the moment. The thorns and thistles of life, the pain and anguish caused by disease, by natural disasters—earthquakes, plagues, and all the rest of the terrors to which we are subject—are not under our dominion even if, through science, we understand more and more about them. There are severe limitations on human dominion at the present time. Perhaps what was meant by those strange passages in Genesis 3 and 9 (see above, "From What Are We Saved?") was that precisely because of our sinful condition, our dominion is now curtailed. We might be much more dangerous to the rest of creation if we had now the full place God intends for us. Only a redeemed humanity can be trusted to have full dominion over the rest of creation.

The passage from Hebrews points to the role of Jesus Christ in the restoration of our human position. Jesus is not only God's unique Son, and therefore fully God; he is also human, also one of us. Though we do not have the dominion intended for us, he does have it. He is now at the right hand of God—that is, sharing God's own power—and yet he continues to be one of us. So we can look at the risen and ascended Christ and see that he is, in a sense, holding our place for us. He is fully the human being God intended us to be. But until redemption is complete in us, until the work of salvation is finished, we can look at Jesus and see our own future. For those who are in Christ, our future is made known by his present. Think again of the passages from the gospels mentioned earlier, where Jesus is pictured as calming the storm and healing the sick. From the point of view of this passage in Hebrews, in these events Jesus is exercising already, in the midst of our fallen world, the dominion that was intended for humanity.

This passage makes it clear that the restoration of full human dominion depends on salvation gained for us by the incarnation, death, and ascension of Jesus. He was equal with God, but for our sake "for a little while was made lower than the angels," that is, he became a human being. Now he is crowned with glory and honor. He tasted death for everyone, and in overcoming death, brought us salvation.

## The Work of the Savior

The redemptive work of Jesus began with his incarnation. We see this in the words of the angel to Mary at the annunciation (Luke 1:30–33), in the words to the shepherds at his birth (Luke 2:10–11), in the words of Simeon at the presentation in the Temple (Luke 2:28–32). His ministry shows his concern for all of life, and his actions of healing show that he is indeed the Lord of creation, undoing the damage human sinfulness has caused in that creation. But his battle with the power of sin sent him to the cross, where evil appeared to have won. It is in the resurrection that the power of death is overcome. He tasted death for everyone, because in his death, he broke the power of sin. For those who are in Christ, who know what he has done and believe the gospel, the power of sin and death have been broken. Now it is possible to begin to live the life God intends for us.

Jesus is not simply an example of what we can be, or a messenger of good news about God's love for us. He is both of these, but that is not what we mean by redemption. Often in the church we have been tempted to reduce his role to these. Particularly when there has been severe conflict between scientific understandings and the message of the Bible, Jesus has been viewed as a human being who has discovered the secret of life, and shares that with us. He has been seen as a teacher. His life is a model. But the church confesses much more than this. Jesus is our redeemer, our savior, because in his death and resurrection he actually overcame—ended the power of—sin and death. Something happened at that moment that changed everything. Something happened, something that Jesus accomplished, or that God accomplished in Jesus. It was something that only God could do, and the power of sin over creation was broken.

It is only by faith that we know this redemption has occurred. The world around us looks the same. Sin and death are still present. But faith knows that the real victory has been won. The decisive battle has occurred. When early Christians needed encouragement to face persecution, John of Ephesus wrote down his vision in what we know as the Revelation to John, the last book of the New Testament. In it he describes a vision of a battle in heaven itself, a battle between the archangel Michael and the dragon—Satan. Satan was defeated, and thrown out of heaven, only to land on the earth. John says that then "I heard a loud voice in heaven, proclaiming. . . . 'Rejoice then, you heavens and those who dwell in them! But woe to the earth and the sea, for the devil has come down to you with great wrath, because he knows that his time is short!' " (Rev. 12:10, 12). In other words, the power of evil has lost the major battle. Its defeat is certain. But now it is even more violent because it knows it is losing. It has been cornered. This is the same sentiment we find in Luther's famous hymn "A Mighty Fortress Is Our God":

The prince of darkness grim,
    We tremble not for him;
His rage we can endure,
    For lo! his doom is sure,
One little word shall fell him.[2]

John of Patmos not only understood the difficulties under which the creation now labors; he also gave us the great vision of the new creation in its fullness. He saw a vision of not only a heavenly life, but also the life of a new earth, complete with the life in a city (Rev. 21:1–2). The fullness of salvation involves a new creation, a new community living in peace and harmony, a creation in which all of the Great Ends of the Church find their fulfillment. There is protection and nurture, spiritual fellowship, worship, truth, social righteousness, and the full, no longer provisional, reality of the kingdom of heaven.

## The Christian Life

If salvation implies not only a word about life after death, but the actual participation in the new creation now, what does such a life look like? The New Testament gives us many clues. Jesus tells us we will have peace, a peace that is very different from the contentment this world can give (John 14:27). We will have joy, a joy that is also given by Christ himself (John 15:11).

In this world, in the life of the old creation, both joy and peace exist. The words exist in secular vocabularies. We experience both of these emotions when things go well, when we feel secure, when we see no storm clouds on the horizon. There is peace when strife has been overcome. There is joy when that for which we had hoped comes to pass: the birth of a child, recovery of a loved one from illness, the completion of some great task. Peace and joy are experienced by human beings all over the world, in all of the world's religions, and even by those who are nonreligious.

The peace and the joy of which the New Testament speaks are of a different character. They are products of the new creation. They are part of the risen life that begins now. Such peace and joy are not dependent on external circumstances. Christians can experience peace even when tragedy strikes. They can know joy when nothing seems to be going well. Both peace and joy in this sense are not the products of this world, but the experience of the abundant life in Christ, a foretaste of that new creation in the midst of the old.

The connection between the life of the new creation and the old is the Holy Spirit. The New Testament often describes the Spirit as the pledge, the down payment, the earnest money of the new creation, which we experience even now: "But it is God who establishes us with you in Christ and has anointed us, by putting his seal on us and giving us his Spirit in our hearts as a first installment" (2 Cor. 1:22; cf. vs. 12–22). And: "In Christ we have also obtained an inheritance. . . . In him you also, when you had heard the word of truth, the gospel of your salvation, and had believed in him, were marked with the seal of the promised Holy Spirit; this is the pledge of our inheritance toward redemption as God's own people" (Eph. 1:11a, 13–14a). The work of the Holy Spirit is the beginning of the new creation even now, in the midst of this old, fallen world. The "fruits" of the Holy Spirit in our lives include the joy and peace that are beyond anything this world can give. According to Paul, "the fruit of the Spirit is love, joy, peace, patience, kindness, generosity, faithfulness, gentleness, and self-control" (Gal. 5:22–23). These are characteristics that overcome the effects of sin on human behavior.

The work of the Holy Spirit creates the church. The fruits of the Spirit lead to community. In fact, without these fruits, human community can be divisive and frustrating. A community without love, patience, goodness, and kindness is not a pleasant place to be. These positive qualities are traits that push us to be with others. There is no way we can be kind, patient, and loving without other people with whom to interact. The church therefore is human community beginning to live as God intended us to live together, a characteristic another Great End of the Church will discuss.

Many Presbyterians have a very limited view of the work of the Holy Spirit. They associate the gifts of the Holy Spirit with more extreme charismatic Christian branches of the church. But we often expect little or nothing in our own lives. When we do this, however, we assume what Paul calls the gifts of the Spirit are virtues that Christians practice on the basis of their own strength. It is helpful to understand that the Holy Spirit is the beginning of the new creation in us, and that the work of the Spirit is to draw us into the community that is the first installment of that new creation.

## Hope

What the church offers in the gospel it proclaims is, above all, hope. In a world in which peace is easily shattered and joy is fleeting, the church offers a joy and peace that cannot be destroyed. In a world that often seems cruel and senseless, the church offers a message of victory. In a world where evil often appears to have the last word, the church proclaims that God in Christ has overcome evil.

It has been said that Christians are short-term pessimists but long-term optimists. We are well aware that there is evil and violence, not only in the world around us, but also in ourselves. Many negative and terrible things can happen. We know that there is illness and disease, disasters that no one can prevent, that cause tragedy and loss. We cannot look at the world around us and assume that everything is going to work out well in the immediate future—or even the future that is within our lifetime. Christians have a very realistic view of this world; they are often more realistic than those who do not know God. For these reasons, we can be quite pessimistic about what is going to happen.

At the same time, we also know that pessimism about God's creation cannot be the last word. Whatever happens, we are the creatures of a good and loving God who, at great cost, has redeemed the world. Evil does not and will not have the last word. For that reason, we can have great hope about the ultimate future—and we know that we will be part of that future.

Hope is not only a matter of feeling good about things. Those who are hopeless cease to work toward any goal, cease to strive to make things better now. They overlook opportunities for healing relationships, for improving their lives or the lives of others, because nothing really matters: there is no hope. Hopelessness is rampant in our world. What the church offers and, in order really to be the church, must offer, is the word of hope based on the redemption of the world through Jesus Christ. Because of Christ, we can have hope about ourselves, about our friends and relatives, about our communities, about our whole world. Medical science can sometimes offer hope that someone will be cured. But even those who are cured will eventually die. There is no escape from that human eventuality. Medical science can extend life expectancy, but it cannot end the reign of death.

Parents who have to deal with a child who has made all the wrong choices, and now suffers the consequences, often feel hopeless. Husbands or wives who face the loss of a spouse, and do not see how they can cope, need hope. Young people who have become addicted to drugs and think that there is no future need hope. Adults who have lost a job and are not sure where to go next need hope.

The Christian message is not only for those who are in the midst of hard times and difficulties. Even those who seem to have everything going their way need the kind of hope that cannot be taken away. Those who give their lives to small goals, who think of success only in terms of income and status, need hope. The list eventually includes all of us. What the gospel offers is a challenge to those who are satisfied with their lives and have settled for too little. Their lives could count for much more. They are much more important in God's world than they ever imagined. Remember the words at the beginning of 1 Peter:

> Blessed be the God and Father of our Lord Jesus Christ! By
> his great mercy he has given us a new birth into a living
> hope through the resurrection of Jesus Christ from the
> dead, and into an inheritance that is imperishable,
> undefiled, and unfading, kept in heaven for you, who are
> being protected by the power of God through faith for a
> salvation ready to be revealed in the last time. *(1 Peter 1:3–5a)*

This perspective of the breadth of God's salvation through Christ is the common understanding in the early church. By the Middle Ages, salvation had been reduced to the future condition of individuals, and the rest of the world seemed unrelated to salvation. Most of the confessions of faith we find in our *Book of Confessions* point to God's creation of the world, and to the fall of human beings. Redemption deals only with human beings. However, more recent theology is again expanding the understanding of salvation, partly because of biblical studies that clearly challenge our narrower vision. The Confession of 1967 reclaims this vision:

> God's redeeming work in Jesus Christ embraces the
> whole of man's [sic] life: social and cultural, economic
> and political, scientific and technological, individual and
> corporate. It includes man's [sic] natural environment as
> exploited and despoiled by sin. It is the will of God that
> his purpose for human life shall be fulfilled under the rule
> of Christ and all evil be banished from his creation. *(BC,* 9.53)

The proclamation of the gospel is the proclamation of hope. Hope and salvation are closely related. If Jesus has broken the power of sin, then new lives are possible for believers. If Jesus has opened the way to a new creation, then there is hope for the transformation of all things that are out of accord with God's will for the world. Real newness is possible because of the death and resurrection of Jesus Christ. This is a message the whole world needs, and the church is entrusted with its proclamation.

---

Notes
1. John Calvin, *Institutes of the Christian Religion* 1.14.8, ed. John T. McNeill, trans. Ford Lewis Battles (Philadelphia: Westminster Press, 1960).

2. Martin Luther, "A Mighty Fortress Is Our God," *The Presbyterian Hymnal* (Louisville, Ky.: Westminster/John Knox Press, 1990), no. 260.

## Study Questions

1. Why has our tradition continued closely to relate Christ's actual death on the cross to human salvation? What has been the value of this? In what ways is our understanding of the means of our salvation changing? In what ways does it stay the same?

2. What does the notion of "being saved" omit? Why does it feel so safe? How does our North American culture color this expression of salvation?

3. Over the centuries, many images of Christ as Savior and of salvation have developed. With which images are you familiar? Which ones do you like? Which ones feel odd?

4. Why should we live moral lives if doing so will not make the world whole again?

5. González states that although God did not wish the world to be corrupt, God intentionally made the result of sin painful. As a result of our sin, we have to live in a world that is estranged from God. How do you respond to this statement?

6. Based on what you recall from Scripture and the Reformed tradition, what is the relation between illness and sin? Have you ever found yourself wondering why tragedies happen to people who don't seem to deserve them? González writes that "a great deal of human misery and sickness is not related to our personal actions." What does this imply for the way we understand salvation?

7. How do you describe the relationship between modern science and the Bible?

8. Have you ever prayed for healing that did not happen? How do you react to Paul's words from 2 Corinthians 12:7b–9a?

9. How can Christ save the natural world? What will be the human role in the process of the world's redemption?

10. González says, "Jesus is not simply an example of what we can be, or a messenger of good news about God's love for us. He is both of these, but that is not what we mean by redemption." What is the problem when we reduce Christ's role to one of these?

11. González states that the joy and peace that characterize the new creation are not dependent on external circumstances. Think back to times when you felt great joy or peace. Do you think that she is right?

12. González says that "the work of the Holy Spirit is the beginning of the new creation" in us. How might the Spirit's presence be freeing? How might it be demanding?

# 4

# The Salvation of Humankind

This first Great End of the Church states that the gospel is proclaimed so that humankind can be saved. Does this mean all of the human race? To whom is salvation offered? For whom is it effective? This directly raises the question of predestination. For generations, Presbyterians have been asked how they can possibly believe such a thing as predestination, which appears to limit salvation rather drastically. Very often, neither the questioner nor the Presbyterian queried has a clear idea what predestination means, and usually the church member responds that she or he does not believe any such thing, nor does anyone in their church! This is probably the case.

However, we need to be very clear about what the Reformed tradition has understood, and what is at stake in this doctrine. It is closely related to the issue of who is included in this offer of salvation. There have been times in the Reformed tradition when some understandings have created serious problems, and we need to look at those as well. It is a doctrine easily misunderstood and misused.

Two very different questions have led to the assertion of the doctrine of predestination. First, how is it that some who hear the gospel respond and others do not? Second, what about all the people who have never really heard the gospel at all? We shall look at both of these issues. They are not new to our generation or even to recent centuries. Christians have raised both questions in some form in all generations. Sometimes very simple answers have been given, most of which have proven unsatisfactory once they were looked at very seriously.

Therefore, in this chapter we shall look at the doctrine of predestination, the issues involved, the opposing opinions, and the unanswered questions that remain. We will also point toward ways of living with the tensions that are inevitably involved in the human understanding of God's ways.

# Predestination

The most common misinterpretation of predestination is to confuse it with predeterminism, as though everything that happens in our lives is the direct result of God's activity and we have no real choices about anything. This is not the meaning of predestination. Predestination has to do with destination, that is, with our final place in eternity, not with all of our choices in the midst of our daily lives.

God's sovereignty and providence do govern all things, but God has created creatures who have wills and activities that act as causes of other actions. God is able to work through and around our decisions so that God's purposes will be accomplished, much as a master chess player is able to work around and through the moves of a novice player. What this means is that creatures make real choices. Human beings have wills and responsibility for how they use them. Other creatures also are causes of activity. For instance, weather conditions are caused by interactions of various factors, not by direct action of God; diseases are caused by germs and viruses. Science can rightly investigate these secondary, contingent causes. But such an assertion of secondary causes and free will in actions does not eliminate the doctrine of predestination, which has to do with the final goal God has for creation in general and human creatures in particular.

In spite of clarity on the definition of predestination, there are still serious questions. The stereotype of the doctrine is the view that God has arbitrarily chosen some people for salvation and others for damnation and that nothing we ourselves can do will make any difference in this matter. Granted, the doctrine has sometimes been presented and understood thus. The clearest statements of this understanding are in the Westminster Confession:

> By the decree of God, for the manifestation of his glory, some men and angels are predestinated unto everlasting life, and others fore-ordained to everlasting death.
>
> These angels and men, thus predestinated and fore-ordained, are particularly and unchangeably designed; and their number is so certain and definite that it cannot be either increased or diminished.
>
> Those of mankind that are predestinated unto life, God, before the foundation of the world was laid, according to his eternal and immutable purpose, and the secret counsel

and good pleasure of his will, hath chosen in Christ, unto everlasting glory, out of his free grace and love alone, without any foresight of faith or good works. . . .

As God hath appointed the elect unto glory, so hath he, by the eternal and most free purpose of his will, fore-ordained all the means thereunto. Wherefore they who are elected being fallen in Adam are redeemed by Christ, are effectually called unto faith in Christ by his Spirit working in due season; are justified, adopted, sanctified, and kept by his power through faith unto salvation. . . .

The rest of mankind, God was pleased, according to the unsearchable counsel of his own will, whereby he extendeth or withholdeth mercy as he pleaseth, for the glory of his sovereign power over his creatures, to pass by, and to ordain them to dishonour and wrath for their sin, to the praise of his glorious justice.

(III. 3–7; *BC*, 6.016–.020)

The issue here is stated clearly and baldly. We may well dislike the statements, and we shall see that the church has also had serious concerns about them. However, before we simply reject them out of hand, we need to look at the very important issues that lie behind such apparently questionable statements. The usual alternative to predestination is the simple statement that God offers salvation to all humanity, and those who accept it are saved, whereas those who reject it are damned. Such a view is not only a part of several theological traditions within the wider church, it is also very compatible with our culture. The dominant culture in this country, the culture in which most of our churches live, assumes we are each responsible for our own lives. We are free to make our own decisions. The freedom of the person is a part of the individualism that characterizes our society. The idea that salvation is offered to all in the proclamation of the gospel, but it is up to each person to decide to choose it or not, goes very well with such individualism. The history of revivals in our country also usually includes the idea that we are free to choose salvation. Decisions for Christ, choosing Jesus as our Lord and Savior—such phrases assume that the decision is ours to make: the church is to proclaim the gospel, but then it is up to each individual to choose to accept it.

There are several problems with such an understanding, however. First, there are many in the world who apparently do not have the option—those who have not heard the gospel, for instance. There are people who live in areas where the gospel has not really been proclaimed. There are other areas where the Christian message is not heard well because of political realities. For instance, in areas of the world where there have been religious civil wars—and there have been many such areas in our day—it would be difficult for a Muslim to hear the gospel in any attractive fashion when family members have been killed by Christians on the basis of their religion. The medieval Crusades also left a view of Christianity in the Middle East that is not helpful for Christian missions.

In addition there are, unfortunately, always children who are too young to have heard the gospel, and who die before they are old enough to make any such choice. In other words, the idea that everyone has such a choice is not really true. It may be relatively true for adults who live in countries that are historically predominantly Christian, but it is hardly the dominant situation in the whole world. Is salvation offered to these others on some basis other than their free choice? Or do they forfeit salvation because they are unable to make a choice? If one must choose, then where you are born may be as much of a limitation on salvation as a doctrine of predestination. That would be a kind of geographical predestination. One's possibility of salvation would really depend on where one was born. The universal availability of salvation that each person can choose is not really true—if the gospel is not clearly known to each person on earth.

But more important, do any of us really choose to believe, or do we find ourselves believing the gospel and therefore acknowledge it? Is it ever possible to will oneself to believe something unless the truth of it has already impressed itself upon our minds? Is faith an act of the will?

What our Reformed tradition has said is that no one believes the gospel unless the grace of God is active in their lives. In fact, grace is absolutely necessary in order for us to believe. It is not that we choose grace that is offered, but grace itself shows us the truth of the gospel, which we can therefore no longer deny. The hymn "Amazing Grace" points to this: To go from being blind to beginning to see the love and mercy of God, beginning to understand what God wills for us and our lives, requires the amazing grace of God. We do not will our way to sight if we are blind. Something has to happen to us so that we can see the truth of the gospel and therefore believe it. That something is the grace of God.

We need a grace that can break through our blindness because, in fact, we are blind to God's truth. That is part of the meaning of the fall. That is what we mean by stating that we are all sinful. Our sinfulness is not just that we choose to do what is wrong. It is deeper than that. Rarely do we decide that we are going to do something though we know it is evil. Usually we have convinced ourselves that what we are going to do is the best action under the circumstances, that it is a sensible and reasonable thing to do, that we are an exception to the usual rule that such behavior is wrong. Only later may we admit to ourselves that at some level we knew it was foolish or wrong. Psychologists would call such a way of thinking "rationalization." Faith calls it the result of our sinful nature. It takes God's grace to break through our tendency to rationalize and justify ourselves and our actions.

Our human problem is not only that we do not do what we should. We also do not always clearly see what we should do. Our instincts for self-preservation, our desire to achieve goals we have set for ourselves that may not be God's goals, our fearfulness, all lead us to determine for ourselves what actions should be taken. Left to ourselves, we are unable to see what the really good action would be. Such an inability to see what is the completely good choice, unaffected by self-interest, is what is meant by "total depravity." That does not mean that we are completely, totally sinful, but that every part of us, including our minds, is affected by sin. Therefore every act, every thought, is mixed with sin.

We cannot assume that what we think is good is actually good in the sight of God. Even our consciences need to be formed by the Holy Spirit, by the Word of God, by grace. Grace breaks through our inability, our blindness, showing us what is good, and showing it in such a way that it becomes undeniable and even attractive to us. Because we have a glimpse of the really good choice through the activity of grace, we therefore may choose to do it.

We cannot choose that which we cannot imagine. Grace enlarges our imagination to include, on occasion, the will of God. It is not that God directly alters our will, but God's grace alters our perception of reality. That is partly what is meant by a new creation appearing for those who are in Christ (2 Cor. 5:17). We do not choose our perception of the world. Nor do we choose to change it.

The ability of grace to break through our blindness, to give us new eyes for seeing the world and God's will in it, is what has traditionally been called the "irresistible" character of grace. Because of our blindness, a simple offer of grace is not sufficient. We could not see it to choose it. Grace must alter us in some way before we can choose that which God wills, including the offer of salvation. We choose, but we choose because God has already changed us.

The Reformed tradition therefore challenges the idea that our own decision is the cause of our salvation. We do choose to believe in Jesus Christ, but only because God's irresistible grace has caused us to see Christ truly as the Redeemer. This does not mean that faith is easy. Grace causes us to see the truth of the gospel, but that may only begin our struggle to live by it. However, we cannot deny that we have seen the truth. We will be haunted by it until we acknowledge it.

Predestination means that God's grace must be received in order for faith to develop, and if that grace is received, faith will develop. That is the implication of "irresistibility." Such grace is not given at birth, but rather may be given at any time. Someone could hear the gospel proclaimed for years, and have no response at all until at some point, it all makes sense. This could happen even when there has been a clear rejection of the church's message for years. Think of Paul's experience of being a persecutor of the church until God's grace turned him around (Acts 9:3–19).

There are times in the history of the church when this understanding of the necessity of irresistible grace has been presented in less than helpful ways. Augustine assumed that human beings were created in order to replace the fallen angels. The number was the same as the number of angels that fell, and therefore the redeemed would take their place to fill out the complement of heaven. There was, in a sense, no room for more than this.[1] Based on this understanding, some believed that only 144,000 would be elected for salvation because this was number of redeemed mentioned in the book of Revelation (Rev. 14:1–5).

Calvin himself placed the doctrine of predestination in the section of the *Institutes of the Christian Religion* that dealt with the experience of redemption. He understood this doctrine as the response of the redeemed who knew that it was not their own merits or even their own right choosing that had led them to faith. That is helpful. But Calvin also seemed to assume that some would have to be damned in order to show that God took sin seriously. It was as though God could not both judge and show mercy on the same people. Some were examples of the mercy of God—the elect—and others were the example of the judgment and wrath of God. This is the same view we see in the Westminster Confession, quoted above.

There are serious problems with such a view. In the second century, the church had declared heretical a view proposed by a man named Marcion. Marcion taught that there were two gods. One was the

Proclamation of the Gospel

God of Israel who was judging and demanded righteousness. The other was the God of Jesus Christ who showed love and forgiveness. For Marcion it was not possible for the One who gave the law to forgive those who went against it. The church declared this completely false, not only because it postulated two gods, but because it altered the revealed character of God who is both just and loving. The God of Israel not only gives the law but also shows great love and mercy to Israel. The same God is the God of Jesus, who not only forgives but also leads us to be holy and just. Marcion's view misreads the Old Testament, where God's love and mercy are constantly praised and experienced. It also misreads the New Testament by assuming there is no emphasis on righteousness as the expected response to God's redemption in Christ. It does not help to say that although there is only one God, the same God cannot show justice and mercy to the same people.

In the centuries after Calvin, as mathematical and scientific thought became more dominant in Europe, some within the Reformed tradition considered God's saving grace to be almost quantifiable. If all those whom God chose actually were saved, then Christ's death was only for those who actually benefited from it. There could not be any excess saving power that did not achieve its goal. Grace was almost equated with a force in physics, and therefore it had to be completely spent as a force. From such thinking came the doctrine of "limited atonement"—that is, Christ died not for all but only for the elect. Therefore, all the saving power released by his redemptive activity on the cross achieved its purpose.

These are all serious problems and have made the understanding of predestination more difficult than it needs to be. But in spite of such problems, the issue of the nature of human sinfulness and its consequences for our ability to choose salvation must be remembered.

## Children of Christian Parents

The Reformed tradition makes some sense when we think of those who grow up outside the church and face a clear moment of accepting or rejecting the church and its message. They can well say that only God's grace turned them from those who did not believe the gospel to those who accepted it.

Those who grow up in the church, whose families are Christians, whose friends are Christians, face a different situation. They have grown up in an atmosphere where the gospel is expected to be believed. It is a part of the church culture in which they live. Many have no clear remembrance of making any radical decision. They have always been part of the church. They may never have seriously questioned the truth of the gospel.

Most of us hope our children will grow up in such a situation and find the gospel the normal and expected grounding of their lives. What does grace mean in such a situation? Are children who grow up in the church not blind to the message of God? Does "total depravity" not affect their minds? We know that cannot be the case.

After the Christian church became the dominant and almost the only religious institution of the Roman Empire in the fourth century, the vast majority of people did grow up in the church. By the medieval period in Europe, it was absolutely necessary to agree with what the church taught or else be considered a heretic. (The only group that was exempted from this were the Jews, who were minimally tolerated, and not always that.) The sense of conversion, the experience of grace that transforms a life, was no longer expected—except as a conversion to religious life, that is, to become a monk or a nun. Even after the Protestant Reformation in the sixteenth century, state churches remained the norm. Everyone in the country was expected to belong to the same church, and grow up within it.

Therefore—speaking for those of us who grew up in a society in which the church was a dominant institution, especially in churches that originally were state churches in Europe—we do not usually anticipate a converting experience of grace. We rather assume that what we have been taught all of our lives is the gospel, and there is no need for God to break through our blindness. Such an attitude may allow an easy acculturation of the gospel. That is, whatever the society holds as good, the church agrees with. Whatever the society holds as evil, the church condemns.

One of the most difficult movements to imagine is the conversion of those who already believe themselves to be Christians—and who all their lives have had a basic understanding of the message of the gospel.

The nineteenth century saw serious struggling with this issue of the conversion of those who grow up within the church. Even though the German liberal theologian Friedrich Schleiermacher believed the sense of God's presence should develop along with all the rest of the maturing process for those who grow up in Christian families, he also strongly believed a converting experience was needed. He wrote: "In any given nation a long series of generations, living on the whole in the state of sanctification, has an influence on those that follow, as natural tendencies to passion are mitigated; yet this never is more than an improved form of general sinfulness, and at some point self-knowledge and penitence must enter."[2]

Within the family and the church, the struggle to follow the will of God is not easy. There is always a "cutting edge" where the church and the society around it disagree, and Christians are called to follow the unpopular path. Parents often fail to model to their children the difficult discernment and action that the life of faith requires. Parents—and adults in the congregation—give children the idea that they, the adults, are always sure of what they should do. Faith is not portrayed as difficult, since perhaps it is assumed such uncertainties would confuse children. The church and the surrounding society are often so enmeshed that there is little cutting edge left. Children seldom see their parents—or adults in the congregation—repenting, rejecting actions they have taken. Such repentance might be viewed as weak or improper. Therefore, children grow up in the church without the sort of experience of the gospel that would make growth with constant repentance possible.

Imagine children of church members and adults who are considering church membership actually watching and overhearing a congregation struggling to discern what their faith requires of them, or repenting of an action or inaction that had taken place, and doing so in a loving and serious manner. Such observers would then realize that faith requires constant, lifelong repentance and conversion.

Søren Kierkegaard, a nineteenth-century Danish Lutheran theologian, wrote very harshly about the effect on the life of faith of the assumption that one lived in a Christian culture. This was a theme in many of his writings, but particularly in a collection of essays titled *Attack on Christendom*. Toward the end of his life he wrote a somewhat autobiographical treatise on the reasons for his writings. In this book, *The Point of View for My Work as an Author*, he makes this statement:

> [A]n illusion can never be destroyed directly. . . . If it is an illusion that all are Christians—and if there is anything to be done about it, it must be done indirectly, not by one who vociferously proclaims himself an extraordinary Christian. . . . There is nothing that requires such gentle handling as an illusion, if one wishes to dispel it. . . . This is what is achieved by the indirect method, which, loving and serving the truth, arranges everything dialectically for the prospective captive, and then shyly withdraws . . . so as not to witness the admission which he makes to himself alone before God—that he has lived hitherto in an illusion.[3]

We need to discover educational methods in our congregations whereby children and adults as well can have the frequent experience of discerning the will of God for themselves and the congregation in concrete decision-making. We all need to be clearer about how the new life given to us in the gospel is something other than decent, responsible life in the secular community. This means discussing issues and possible courses of action before they are so politicized that lines are hardened and enmity rather than love are the result. In many congregations, however, there do not seem to be many significant decisions made. What leads to significant decision-making moments is a congregation's strong sense of mission. Mission, especially hands-on, local mission, always requires constant decisions. These will either be made on the basis of discernment or on the basis of practical, secular concerns.

Discernment of the will of God requires God's grace. It is not simply our best thinking. Therefore, the desire for discernment strengthens the life of prayer and Bible study both for a congregation and for individuals. We often underestimate the power of sin in our lives and in our society, and therefore expect the life of faith to be easy. The Reformed tradition has been very clear that faith is not easy. Again, a strong view of sin that includes total depravity goes against the assumption in our society that the individual is free and under no outside power when making decisions.

Discernment of the will of God requires God's grace. It is not simply our best thinking. Therefore, the desire for discernment strengthens the life of prayer and Bible study both for a congregation and for individuals. We often underestimate the power of sin in our lives and in our society, and therefore expect the life of faith to be easy. The Reformed tradition has been very clear that faith is not easy. Again, a strong view of sin that includes total depravity goes against the assumption in our society that the individual is free and under no outside power when making decisions.

It is no accident that the new baptismal ceremonies include the ancient practice of renunciations, that is rejection of the power of sin as a prelude to our acceptance of Christ. Our tradition has been very clear that we are not free agents who simply need to choose to add a confession of faith in Christ. We are bound to ways of thinking, ways of responding, ways of understanding and viewing the world that are strongly affected by sin. We cannot see what God wills without the power of God's grace in our lives. This is as true of our children as it is of those who grow up without hearing the gospel. Turning our lives toward God involves the commitment to turn away from the ways of sin.

# The Heart of the Difficulty

Whether we think of children of believers or adults who come to faith from outside the church, there remains a serious difficulty. To put it in the harshest terms: If we believe that God's grace is absolutely necessary in order for us to hear and respond to the gospel, and that God's grace ultimately will accomplish what it seeks to do, then we are left with serious questions about those who do not hear the gospel, or hearing it, do not respond. How can we say, in the first Great End, that the proclamation of the gospel is for the salvation of humankind if what we really mean is that it is for the salvation of a limited number of people to whom God chooses to give the needed grace?

We cannot assume that other generations of Christians saw no problem and only we, in our enlightened age, have discovered the difficulties. There has been within the Christian tradition a constant balancing of the seriousness of sin in human life and the loving and merciful character of God. It often appears that to preserve the loving character of God we have to assume that human beings are quite free to choose the grace that God offers. In the case of those who never hear the gospel, we decide that belief in Christ is only for those who hear the gospel and God works in some other way with those in other religions. The Reformed tradition has historically opposed these conclusions on biblical grounds: First, Christ is God's redemptive plan for all people. There is no different plan for those who have not heard the gospel. Second, the power of sin is too strong to permit human beings to see that grace and choose it: grace must break into their lives and understandings and change them before it can be effective.

Perhaps the clearest statement of the difficulty was penned more than a millennium ago. It is usually ascribed to a man named Prosper of Aquitaine, who was a layman, a monk in southern Gaul in the fifth century. There had already been great controversy between St. Augustine of Hippo and the British monk Pelagius. In the beginning of the fourth century, Augustine had put forth the strongest argument yet as to the overwhelming nature of sin in human life and the necessity of irresistible grace to overcome the power of sin. This had led to the first clear formulation of what we know as the doctrine of predestination. Pelagius had emphasized the freedom of the human will to do that which God required, and de-emphasized the need for grace.

Though many Christians at the time condemned Pelagius, it did not mean that they all agreed with Augustine's conclusions. Many attempted to find some middle way. They stressed the need for grace, but assumed that human beings were free to accept or reject this grace, thus limiting the effects of sin.

It was in the midst of this debate that the treatise *The Call of All Nations,* by Prosper of Aquitaine, appeared. In it we find this statement:

> If we give up completely all wrangling that springs up in the heat of immoderate disputes, it will be clear that we must hold for certain three points concerning the problem. . . . First, we must confess that God wills all men to be saved and to come to the knowledge of truth. Secondly, there can be no doubt that all who actually come to the knowledge of the truth and to salvation, do so not in virtue of their own merits but of the efficacious help of divine grace. Thirdly, we must admit that human understanding is unable to fathom the depths of God's judgments, and we ought not to inquire why He who wishes all men to be saved does not in fact save all.[4]

Prosper does not mince words. He makes very clear the issue and the contradiction. In earlier chapters he had given the biblical witness to both the will of God to save all and the absolute need for God's activity for individuals to be saved. We may not like his solution—that we cannot know how both can be true, and must leave all such matters in the hands of God—but he causes us to face the issues involved without blinking.

In the fourteenth century, Julian of Norwich, an Englishwoman who was an anchoress—that is, a solitary monastic—living in an apartment adjoining the church in Norwich, wrote down the visions she had had during a serious illness years before. In the midst of her delirium, when she was thought to be dying, a crucifix was placed at the foot of her bed where she could see it. During the night she had visions of conversations with Jesus on the cross, conversations in which she asked all sorts of theological questions and received answers. Years later she wrote down both the visions that she had and her understanding of what she had learned. Julian was a faithful medieval woman, not a scholar. She states her beliefs clearly and unambiguously, and understands the difficulty as clearly as did Prosper. She writes:

> Our faith is founded on God's word, and it belongs to our faith that we believe that God's word will be preserved in all things. And one article of our faith is that many creatures will

be damned, such as the angels who fell out of heaven because of pride, who now are devils, and many men upon earth who die out of the faith of Holy Church, that is to say those who are pagans and many who have received baptism and who live unchristian lives and so die out of God's love. All these will be eternally condemned to hell, as Holy Church teaches me to believe.

And all this being so, it seemed to me that it was impossible that every kind of thing should be well, as our Lord revealed at this time. And to this I had no other answer as a revelation from our Lord except this: What is impossible to you is not impossible to me. I shall preserve my word in everything, and I shall make everything well. And in this I was taught by the grace of God that I ought to keep myself steadfastly in the faith, as I had understood before, and that at the same time I should stand firm and believe firmly that every kind of thing will be well, as our Lord revealed at that same time. For this is the great deed which our Lord will do, and in this deed he will preserve his word in everything. And he will make well all which is not well. But what the deed will be and how it will be done, there is no creature who is inferior to Christ who knows it, or will know it until it has been done, according to the understanding which I received of our Lord's meaning at this time.[5]

Julian, like Prosper, is unambiguous about the difficulty, a difficulty which she casts in somewhat different terms than Prosper. The mercy of God for the whole world on the one hand and the number of people who do not follow the way of Christ on the other are put in opposition. Like Prosper, she does not solve the problem. For both writers, it is beyond human ability to discover a solution. We must trust the God whose grace we have experienced.

The Presbyterian Church has also struggled with the conflicts involved in the necessity of God's work in Christ for salvation and the love of God for all people. In 1903 the Presbyterian Church in the United States of America (the larger northern stream of our present denomination) added a chapter XXXV to the Westminster Confession of Faith, as well as a "Declaratory Statement" at the end. In part, the chapter reads:

In the gospel God declares his love for the world and his desire that all men should be saved; reveals fully and clearly the only way of salvation; promises eternal life to all who truly repent and believe in Christ. . . .

It is the duty and privilege of everyone who hears the gospel immediately to accept its merciful provisions; and they who continue in impenitence and unbelief incur aggravated guilt and perish by their own fault. (*BC*, 6.188–.189)[6]

In the Declaratory Statement we find these words:

[W]ith reference to Chapter III of the Confession of Faith; that concerning those who are saved in Christ, the doctrine of God's eternal decree is held in harmony with the doctrine of his love to all mankind, his gift of his Son to be the propitiation for the sins of the whole world, and his readiness to bestow his saving grace on all who seek it; . . . that his decree hinders no man from accepting that offer. . . .

[W]ith reference to Chapter X, Section 3, of the Confession of Faith, that it is not to be regarded as teaching that any who die in infancy are lost. We believe that all dying in infancy are included in the election of grace, and are regenerated, and saved by Christ through the Spirit, who works when and where and how he pleases. (*BC*, 6.192–.193)[7]

It is clear that at the beginning of the twentieth century there was unhappiness with a doctrine of election that seemed to contradict God's love for all. The need for "irresistible grace" was muted, and it was declared that all infants are elect, unless they live to an age when they can decide for themselves. Global mission was a major emphasis in this added chapter, and the doctrine of election was seen as endangering mission. This chapter of the Westminster Confession shows that the gospel needs to be proclaimed throughout the world so that everyone can make a decision and supports the view that we are free to make a decision for Christ. Having heard the gospel, it is a person's own fault if he or she does not choose to believe. (Note also the astonishing statement that all children who die in infancy are among the elect. What is surprising is that this statement makes no distinction between children of believers and other children, which would lead to the conclusion that those children who live in an area where the gospel has not been preached would be saved if they died in infancy but condemned if they lived to an age of accountability and did not believe the gospel.)

On many grounds, these statements are a move away from historic Reformed beliefs. It shows the influence of the culture of the United States with its emphasis on individual freedom. The difficulties still remain, however, because such freedom does not exist for many people, and the effects of sin and therefore the need for grace are seriously downplayed.

We are generally not satisfied with unsolved intellectual problems. We want answers that satisfy us and can be given to others who question us. The difficulties we see can be viewed in two ways that are not incompatible. First, when the kingdom comes, we may very well discover that we human beings have defined matters such as grace and free will in ways that are not accurate. We may have assumed we understood the redemptive work of God more completely than we really have and therefore hardened lines of argument that should have been left considerably fuzzier. Second, even in the midst of a scientific, modern world, we must leave room for mystery. Faith and doctrine are not the same. We have experienced the love and mercy of a God who loves the whole creation. This same God is righteous and takes sin very seriously. We have also experienced the redemptive work of Christ and believe that he is the unique Redeemer of the world. All these truths are attested to in Scripture. How it can be that a righteous God is also forgiving? How—and whether—Christ redeems those whom we do not see as related to him we cannot know. Thankfully, their salvation does not depend on our understanding. God's redemptive work does not wait until we can solve the intellectual difficulties. Our task is to live by what we do understand.

The first approach, namely, that we have defined God's grace and human free will in false ways is given some support by Scripture itself. When we choose one side—either God's grace as totally determinative for redemption or human choice as the ultimate factor—we do detriment to the other. That is, if we choose to emphasize human choice in regard to the gospel, then we downplay the effects of sin in our lives, and the consequent need for the work of grace. If we emphasize our dependence on grace, then we may do serious damage to the understanding of the universality of God's love.

What is interesting is that the Gospel of John can readily be used to support both positions. For instance, if one were to seek confirmation of the idea that we are free to choose God's offer of salvation, then verses such as these could be cited:

> But to all who received him, who believed in his name, he gave power to become children of God. (John 1:12)
>
> "For God so loved the world that he gave his only Son, so that everyone who believes in him may not perish but may have eternal life." (John 3:16)
>
> "Anyone who resolves to do the will of God will know whether the teaching is from God or whether I am speaking on my own." (John 7:17)
>
> "I have come as light into the world, so that everyone who believes in me should not remain in the darkness. I do not judge anyone who hears my words and does not keep them, for I came not to judge the world, but to save the world. The one who rejects me and does not receive my word has a judge; on the last day the word that I have spoken will serve as judge." (John 12:46–48)

All of these point in the direction that we must choose. Whether we believe in Jesus and the gospel he proclaims is up to us.

At the same time, were we to take the position of Calvin and Augustine, we would have great support in a passage such as this:

> "Do not be astonished that I said to you, 'You must be born from above.' The wind blows where it chooses, and you hear the sound of it, but you do not know where it comes from or where it goes. So it is with everyone who is born of the Spirit." (John 3:7–8)

Or several passages in John 6:

> "Everything that the Father gives me will come to me, and anyone who comes to me I will never drive away; for I have come down from heaven, not to do my own will, but the will of him who sent me. And this is the will of him who

sent me, that I should lose nothing of all that he has given me, but raise it up on the last day." (John 6:37–39)

"No one can come to me unless drawn by the Father who sent me; and I will raise that person up on the last day." (John 6:44)

"It is the spirit that gives life. . . . But among you there are some who do not believe." For Jesus knew from the first who were the ones that did not believe, and who was the one that would betray him. And he said, "For this reason I have told you that no one can come to me unless it is granted by the Father." (John 6:63a, 64–65)

In later chapters of John there are also passages that point to the need for God's action in order for a person to believe:

"[Y]ou do not believe, because you do not belong to my sheep. My sheep hear my voice. I know them, and they follow me. I give them eternal life, and they will never perish. No one will snatch them out of my hand." (John 10:26–28)

"You did not choose me but I chose you." (John 15:16a)

"I have made your name known to those whom you gave me from the world. They were yours, and you gave them to me, and they have kept your word. Now they know that everything you have given me is from you; for the words that you gave to me I have given to them, and they have received them and know in truth that I came from you; and they have believed that you sent me." (John 17:6–8)

All of these passages point in a very different direction than the ones cited earlier. What shall we do about such apparent contradictions? It would be easier if these passages were in different books of the Bible, or by different authors. But they are in the same book, penned by the same author. The wisest thing to do is probably to assume that we have so defined the issue in our own day—and for several centuries—that we have lost some perspective that was clear to much earlier generations. We have been forced to choose, whereas somehow the truth includes both our decision and the essential action of God's Spirit in order for us to choose.

It is interesting that in two of the earlier Reformed documents to be found in our *Book of Confessions*, the Scots Confession and the Heidelberg Catechism, though the stress is on the absolute inability of sinful human beings to come to faith without the grace of God breaking though the effects of sin, the issue of predestination is not emphasized. These documents were written in 1560 and 1562. The Second Helvetic Confession was written in 1561, and deals with the topic rather fully, but with clear warnings as to the dangers involved in the doctrine, and clear limitations on what we can know of the will of God. It is not until we come to the seventeenth century document, the Westminster Confession, that we see the centrality of the doctrine in our confessional statements. The later documents, the Theological Declaration of Barmen (1934), the Confession of 1967, and the Brief Statement of Faith (1983), do not deal directly with the issue.

## The Purpose of Election

The proclamation of the gospel is for the salvation of humankind. We proclaim the gospel because it is the good news of what God has done for all the world in the life, death, and resurrection of Jesus Christ. Whenever the people of God stress the fact that they have been chosen by God, there is always the danger that they will consider this a sign that they are better than others, or that God loves them more than others. But it is clear that the choosing is for a task. We have been chosen as the church for the task of proclamation. God is concerned for more than us. If this were not so, there would be no need for the church. God's concern for the world is what has caused the church to come into existence. We have been chosen for mission and not for privilege.

The Second Helvetic Confession also points to sanctification as the task of the elect: "Finally, the saints are chosen in Christ by God for a definite purpose, which the apostle himself explains when he says, 'He chose us in him for adoption that we should be holy and blameless before him in love'" (*BC*, 5.054).

The mission of the church, the task given to it, is both proclamation and sanctification. These are not really two separate tasks, but they demonstrate the connection between what we say with our lips and what we show by our lives. Sanctification is the process of becoming holy, of living ever more closely to the way God created us to live. It is the work of the Holy Spirit within us.

We often assume that sanctification is an individual task, that we are each to become holier. But that is not the biblical view. Constantly in the perspective of the biblical writers is the holy community, the people of God, who by their life together show the world how we are to live. If we are to be believable in our proclamation, our life as a community of faith must also show signs of the work of the Spirit in our midst.

As we saw in chapter 3, God's concern for the world is for more than humankind. If human beings take their rightful place, obedient and thankful to God their creator, then the rest of creation will experience its own form of salvation. Exactly how God will use our work is not our problem. We have been gathered as the church for the task of proclamation. That is what we must do. We must leave the results to God. We cannot control the work of the Holy Spirit.

Can the church really be the church without engaging in the mission of proclamation? Evidently not. Furthermore, a church that really seeks to carry out its mission will be renewed. There is something about seeing the effect of faith in the lives of others that renews our own. If our proclamation reaches fertile soil, that is, hearts prepared by the Holy Spirit, then we can see faith begin to blossom and flourish in other people and our own faith is strengthened.

Presbyterians are often tempted to limit their proclamation to those who already lead basically "good" lives. We assume that those who are clearly and publicly sinful, or have made such terrible choices that their lives are seriously disordered, are not interested in what we have to say. We may help them, but our mission may well be limited to such help, without any real proclamation.

For instance, a church that has a soup kitchen or a night shelter may well assume its mission is to meet the physical or even social needs of the people who come. But the thought that they might become members of our congregation is not part of our agenda. Why? Were we to see the gospel radically transform their lives, what effect would it have on our own faith? Often our rationale is that they would not be comfortable in our worship. But it is probably equally true that we are the ones who would not be comfortable. Why? Would we be uncomfortable with those for whom the gospel has been a matter of life and death, for whom it has caused an enormous transformation? Might we wonder why the gospel has not had such a great effect in our own lives? Do we really expect that the gospel can transform lives? Do our own lives need transformation by the gospel? What would it look like? These are all questions that a congregation needs to struggle with when it asks who the people are to whom it is to proclaim the gospel.

To witness, to proclaim, is to risk being changed ourselves. If faith has no power in the lives of others, there is no point in proclaiming it. If it does have great power, we must be ready to have that power unleashed in our own lives.

In chapter 2, we looked at what happened to the church when it became the dominant religion of the Roman Empire. Increasingly, being a Christian was equated with being a decent, upright citizen. Such citizens also assumed that they of course believed what the church taught. But belief was frequently a surface acceptance of teachings, not the source of a transformation of life. Why would one need such a transformation if one were already a decent and good person? That is very much the situation we have inherited in our churches in this country. But such a view is strongly challenged today. It is challenged on two fronts.

First, we are discovering that there are many people who are decent, upright citizens who are not part of the church. They volunteer to help others, they are concerned about problems in the community. They are generous in their support of civic projects. Such people may be part of other religious groups or they may be totally secular. How do Christians differ from them?

Second, many people within our churches are seeking greater involvement, greater study, greater commitment. Are they looking for the transformation that the gospel promises? How can we regain the sense of new life, of being part of a new creation, that the early church clearly understood? They are asking the question, What does it mean to be a Christian?

There is a strange contradiction built into the nature of the church. It is difficult to carry out mission if we are not clear about the power of the gospel in our own lives. At the same time, we cannot experience that power if we are not engaged in mission. A congregation cannot wait to be about the task of proclamation until it has fully experienced the power of the gospel for itself, nor will its proclamation be powerful if it does not stem from the reality the congregation has experienced.

Though this is true, we need to remember that the power to convince others does not come from us; it comes from the Holy Spirit. We must begin both processes at the same time, and continue both processes throughout our lives and the life of a congregation. That is, we always need to gain greater understanding of the meaning of the gospel. This comes from Bible study, from the study of our confessional documents, from engaging in the disciplines of the devotional life, from the worship of the gathered community. All of these need to be done, and we can expect no time of completion, of finishing with this and then going on to proclaim the gospel to others.

On the other hand, we must be about mission that includes proclamation. This means beginning where we are as a congregation, whether strongly engaged or barely started. The German theologian Dietrich Bonhoeffer, who was imprisoned and killed by the Nazi government, describes this almost contradictory process in a little book called *The Cost of Discipleship*. In it he describes how individuals renew their faith. His words can apply equally well to the life of a congregation:

> This situation may be described by two propositions, both of which are equally true. Only he who believes is obedient, and only he who is obedient believes. . . . Not only do those who believe obey, but only those who obey believe. In the one case faith is the condition of obedience, and in the other obedience the condition of faith.[8]

If we are to believe, we must obey a concrete command. Without this preliminary step of obedience, our faith will only be pious humbug, and will lead us to the grace that is not costly. Everything depends on the first step. It has a unique quality of its own. The first step of obedience makes Peter leave his nets, and later get out of the boat; it calls upon the young man to leave his riches. Only this new existence, created through obedience, can make faith possible.[9] If a congregation seeks the sort of renewal that shows the power of salvation and prepares it for joyful proclamation in its mission to the world, then it must obey what it already knows of the will of God for its life together, however small a step that might be. It might be to begin a prayer group, seeking God's will for the congregation. It might be a Bible study, not simply an objective study but one in which the members covenant to implement what they discover, that gives direction to their congregational life. It might be a specific mission in the wider community in which the congregation seeks to proclaim its faith. What matters is that it is a step taken in obedience to what is understood as God's call to this congregation.

An obedient congregation is ready to engage in proclamation. To be a congregation ready and able to proclaim the gospel for the salvation of humankind is to be the church in its exciting fullness. Proclamation becomes the engine for the renewal of the church that is proclaiming. It renews in the congregation the meaning of the gospel and the experience of salvation. It is a very good place to begin a study of the Great Ends of the Church.

## Notes

1. Augustine, *Enchiridion in Augustine: Confessions and Enchiridion*, ed. and trans. Albert C. Outler, The Library of Christian Classics, vol. VII (Philadelphia: The Westminster Press, 1955), pp. 355–359; *The City of God*, trans. Henry Bettenson (London: Penguin Books, 1984), p. 22.
2. Friedrich Schleiermacher, *The Christian Faith*, trans. and ed. From the 2nd German edition by H. R. Mackintosh and J. S. Stewart (Edinburgh: T. & T. Clark, 1928), p. 538.
3. Søren Kierkegaard, *The Point of View for My Work as an Author*, trans. Walter Lowrie (New York: Harper & Row, Harper Torchbooks, 1962), pp. 24–26.
4. Prosper of Acquitaine, *The Call of All Nations*, trans. P. de Letter, Ancient Christian Writers: The Works of the Fathers in Translation, no. 14 (New York: Newman Press, 1952), p. 89.
5. Julian of Norwich, *Showings*, trans. Edmund Colledge and James Walsh, The Classics of Western Spirituality (New York: Paulist Press, 1978), p. 233.
6. The Westminster Confession, chap. XXXV, *Book of Confessions* (Louisville, KY: Office of the General Assembly, Presbyterian Church (U.S.A.), 2002), 6.188–.189.
7. The Westminster Confession, chap. XXXV, Declaratory Statement, *Book of Confessions*, 6.192–.193.
8. Dietrich Bonhoeffer, *The Cost of Discipleship*, trans. R. H. Fuller (New York: Macmillan Co., 1955), p. 56.
9. Ibid.

# Study Questions

1. How would you describe God's sovereignty? What have our confessions said about God's sovereign power?

2. Why does our tradition insist that free will of the human creature is real? How is human freedom circumscribed, or limited? How do you react to the portion of the Westminster Confession (III. 3-7) cited at the beginning of this chapter?

3. Describe the work of the Holy Spirit in human salvation. In what ways does it leave decisions to individuals? In what ways does the Holy Spirit "override" human freedom?

4. If we cannot avoid doing wrong despite our best intentions, why should we aim for the good?

5. What is the true meaning of irresistible grace? Of predestination?

6. What are the problems with Marcion's view of the Scriptures?

7. Scientific and other forms of cultural thought inevitably flavor theological interpretations. González discusses the limitations of Augustine's scientific perspective and Calvin's own interpretation of the meaning of predestination. What might be some examples today of this same phenomenon?

8. In what way is conscious decision important and even necessary for the growth of faith in North America? Does life in your congregation feel like a commitment? If so, in what ways? How can the members of a congregation become more intentional in serving Christ with their lives?

9. What does the Reformed tradition say about those who never hear the gospel? What does González say is wrong with the assumption that God works in different ways in religions other than Christianity? What is your response?

10. How do you respond to Prosper's solution? Which solution do you favor, Prosper's or Julian's?

11. Universal salvation seems to unify God's love and God's judgment, while the doctrine of predestination, interpreted as the election of a few to salvation and the rest to damnation, pits divine love and mercy against each other. Why is the truth of God's irresistible grace, as González has described it on page 76, so important here?

12. How does González describe our election? The mission of the church? What are the risks involved?

# Postscript

We have looked rather extensively at the meaning of this first Great End of the Church: "the proclamation of the gospel for the salvation of humankind." Having done this, we are in a position to look again at the connection of all of the Great Ends.

Let us look at the second Great End: "the shelter, nurture, and spiritual fellowship of the children of God." If a congregation is really ready to proclaim the gospel to others, it will, in its own internal life, be "a spiritual fellowship of the children of God." Lone evangelists and members of a congregation who individually take on the task of evangelism when the congregation as a whole does not may not depend on the character of the congregation for their support. But the text of the Great Ends of the Church assumes that these are congregational goals, not individual tasks. Nor can the lone evangelist invite others into a vital church if the congregation as a whole is not ready for them. All of us need the "shelter and nurture" which the congregation, as the "spiritual fellowship of the children of God," provides. This first Great End depends upon the second both as the source of its support and the home for those who, because of the proclamation, are moved by the Spirit to join the fellowship of the congregation.

The third Great End is "the maintenance of divine worship." Those who understand that it is not their own strength and goodness that has brought them the fruits of salvation will worship God willingly and gratefully. If there is no desire to worship God, if that is not the joyful center of the life of the community of faith, then there is no basis for proclamation. The sacraments renew our faith. They bring us to the heart of the gospel itself, without which we tend to proclaim ourselves rather than Christ. Proclamation and worship go together. The worship service itself, centering on the Word and the sacraments, is proclamation within the community to prepare it to proclaim to those outside of the community.

The fourth Great End is "the preservation of the truth." A congregation that has a very limited view of the gospel, that fails to see what astonishing good news it is for our world, will have a difficult time proclaiming anything of interest to the world. There is always the temptation to tailor the gospel so completely to what is already believable by our society that the gospel is no news at all. At the same time, the truth cannot be stated once and for all and then merely repeated century after century. We must reappropriate the gospel in our own lives, both individually and congregationally, and through our study of the Scripture be ready to proclaim the truth of the gospel that is indeed good news.

The fifth Great End is "the promotion of social righteousness." In terms of proclamation, such promotion is partly the necessary sanctification of the congregation that is the proclamation by its life in the world. We have also seen that the work of salvation is not only for individuals, but also has to do with God's concern for the whole of creation. To speak of social righteousness is to speak of the public voice of the church, the proclamation of the gospel beyond its impact on private lives.

The last of the Great Ends is "the exhibition of the Kingdom of Heaven to the world." This is the work of the sanctification of the congregation, the witness of the church's life in the wider community. But it is also the proclamation of hope in a world that tends to despair, a word that this remains God's creation, and God's will for the world will be accomplished. Hope because we know of God's love and mercy, seen above all in the Christ Jesus, is central to our proclamation.

Just as we can see that this first Great End of the Church has implications for all of the others, we can also anticipate that studies of these other Great Ends will lead to even more understanding of our purpose as the church to proclaim the gospel. We can, however, increase our obedience on the basis of what we understand now. The world awaits our faithfulness.